Better Homes and Gardens®

delicious soups

Better Homes and Gardens®

delicious
soups

WILEY

John Wiley & Sons, Inc.

John Wiley & Sons, Inc.
Publisher: Natalie Chapman
Associate Publisher: Jessica Goodman
Executive Editor: Anne Ficklen
Production Manager: Michael Olivo
Production Editor: Abby Saul
Cover Design: Suzanne Sunwoo
Art Director: Tai Blanche
Layout: Indianapolis Composition
  Services
Manufacturing Manager: Tom Hyland

Better Homes and Gardens®

Test Kitchen™

Our seal assures you that every recipe in *Delicious Soups* has been tested in the Better Homes and Gardens® Test Kitchen. This means that each recipe is practical and reliable and meets our high standards of taste appeal. We guarantee your satisfaction with this book for as long as you own it.

For general information on our other products and services or for technical support, please contact our Customer Care Department within the United States at (877) 762–2974, outside the United States at (317) 572–3993 or fax (317) 572–4002.

Wiley also publishes its books in a variety of electronic formats. Some content that appears in print may not be available in electronic books. For more information about Wiley products, visit our web site at www.wiley.com.

Library of Congress Cataloging-in-Publication Data is available upon request.

ISBN: 978-1-435-12632-9

Printed in China.

10 9 8 7 6 5 4 3 2 1

contents

chicken
AND TURKEY

Golden Turkey–Split Pea Soup, *page 43*

chicken SOUP WITH SPINACH AND ORZO

Start to Finish: 20 minutes
Makes: 6 servings

- **4 14-ounce cans reduced-sodium chicken broth**
- **1 cup dried orzo**
- **12 ounces fresh asparagus spears, trimmed and bias-sliced into 1½-inch pieces**
- **3 cups chopped fresh spinach, Swiss chard, or kale, or one 10-ounce package frozen chopped spinach, thawed and well drained**
- **1½ cups chopped fresh tomatoes (3 medium)**
- **1½ cups shredded cooked chicken (8 ounces)**
- **⅓ cup cubed cooked ham**
- **Salt and ground black pepper**
- **Snipped fresh chives and/or parsley (optional)**

1 In a covered 5- to 6-quart Dutch oven, bring broth to boiling. Add orzo. Return to boiling; reduce heat. Simmer, uncovered, for 6 minutes. Add asparagus; simmer, for about 2 minutes more or until orzo is tender and asparagus is crisp-tender.

2 Stir in spinach, tomato, chicken, and ham; heat through. Season to taste with salt and pepper. If desired, sprinkle servings with chives.

Nutrition facts per serving: 221 cal., 4 g total fat (1 g sat. fat), 35 mg chol., 837 mg sodium, 28 g carb., 3 g dietary fiber, 20 g protein.

easy CHICKEN NOODLE SOUP

Start to Finish: 30 minutes
Makes: 6 servings

3   **14-ounce cans reduced-sodium chicken broth**

1   **cup chopped onion (1 large)**

1   **cup sliced carrots (2 medium)**

1   **cup sliced celery (2 stalks)**

1   **cup water**

2   **teaspoons dried Italian seasoning, crushed**

½   **teaspoon ground black pepper**

1   **bay leaf**

1   **16-ounce package frozen egg noodles**

2   **cups chopped cooked chicken or turkey (10 ounces)***

2   **tablespoons snipped fresh parsley (optional)**

1 In a large saucepan, combine broth, onion, carrots, celery, the water, Italian seasoning, pepper, and bay leaf. Bring to boiling; reduce heat. Simmer, covered, for 5 minutes.

2 Stir in frozen noodles. Return to boiling; reduce heat. Simmer, covered, for 10 to 12 minutes more or until noodles are tender but still firm and vegetables are just tender. Stir in chicken; heat through.

3 Remove and discard bay leaf. If desired, sprinkle each serving with parsley.

Nutrition facts per serving: 339 cal., 6 g total fat (2 g sat. fat), 130 mg chol., 554 mg sodium, 46 g carb., 3 g dietary fiber, 23 g protein.

*Tip: If you don't have any leftover chicken or turkey, use about half of a 2- to 2¼-pound purchased roasted chicken from the supermarket deli; skin, bone, and chop the meat. Or cook your own chicken. In a large skillet, combine 12 ounces skinless, boneless chicken breast halves and 1½ cups water. Bring to boiling; reduce heat. Simmer, covered, for 12 to 14 minutes or until chicken is no longer pink (170°F). Drain and chop.

chicken-and-vegetable
BEAN SOUP

To save time on early morning preparation, precook the beans the night before, drain at once, rinse, and store in the refrigerator. In the morning, just put them into the slow cooker along with the vegetables and seasonings.

Prep: 25 minutes
Stand: 1 hour
Cook: 8 to 10 hours (low) or 4 to 5 hours (high)
Makes: 4 to 6 servings

1 **cup dried Great Northern beans**

6 **cups cold water**

1 **cup chopped onion**

1 **medium fennel bulb, trimmed and cut into ½-inch pieces**

2 **medium carrots, chopped**

2 **cloves garlic, chopped**

2 **tablespoons chopped fresh parsley**

1 **teaspoon dried rosemary**

¼ **teaspoon ground black pepper**

4½ **cups chicken broth**

2½ **cups shredded or chopped cooked chicken or turkey**

1 **14.5-ounce can diced tomatoes**

1 Rinse beans; drain. In large saucepan, combine beans and the water. Bring to a boil; reduce heat. Simmer, uncovered, for 10 minutes. Remove from heat. Cover and let stand for 1 hour. Drain and rinse beans.

2 Meanwhile, in a 3½- to 5-quart slow cooker, combine onion, fennel, carrots, garlic, parsley, rosemary, and pepper. Place beans on vegetables. Pour chicken broth over contents.

3 Cover and cook on low-heat setting for 8 to 10 hours or on high-heat setting for 4 to 5 hours.

4 If necessary, raise temperature to high-heat setting. Stir in chicken and tomatoes with their juices. Cover slow cooker; cook for about 30 minutes longer or until heated through.

Nutrition facts per serving: 426 cal., 10 g total fat (3 g sat. fat), 78 mg chol., 1454 mg sodium, 46 g carb., 15 g dietary fiber, 40 g protein.

asian CHICKEN NOODLE SOUP

Udon or soba noodles and miso give this soup Asian character. Miso is fermented soybean paste and a common flavoring in Japanese cuisine. Look for both the noodles and miso in Asian markets.

Start to Finish: 20 minutes
Makes: 4 servings

- 2 14-ounce cans reduced-sodium chicken broth
- 1 cup water
- 3 ounces udon or soba noodles, broken in half (1 cup)
- 1 medium red sweet pepper, bias-sliced into bite-size strips (½ cup)
- ⅓ cup sliced scallions
- 1 tablespoon white miso
- 1 tablespoon grated fresh ginger
- ⅛ teaspoon crushed red pepper
- 1½ cups chopped cooked chicken or turkey
- 1 cup fresh snow pea pods, halved crosswise, or ½ of a 6-ounce package frozen snow pea pods, thawed and halved crosswise
- Crushed red pepper (optional)

❶ In a large saucepan, combine broth and water. Bring to boiling. Add noodles. Return to boiling; reduce heat. Simmer, covered, for 6 minutes.

❷ Stir sweet pepper, scallions, miso, ginger, and the ⅛ teaspoon crushed red pepper into broth mixture. Add chicken. Return to boiling; reduce heat. Simmer, covered, for 3 minutes. Stir in pea pods. Simmer, uncovered, for 1 minute more or until pea pods are crisp-tender. Ladle soup into bowls. If desired, sprinkle with crushed red pepper.

Nutrition facts per serving: 225 cal., 6 g total fat (1 g sat. fat), 51 mg chol., 937 mg sodium, 22 g carb., 2 g dietary fiber, 23 g protein.

mexican-style
CHICKEN SOUP

Prep: 30 minutes
Cook: 20 minutes
Makes: 6 servings

- 2 teaspoons canola oil
- 1 large onion, chopped
- 1 large red sweet pepper, seeded and chopped
- 1½ teaspoons chili powder
- 1 teaspoon ground cumin
- 2 14-ounce cans reduced-sodium chicken broth
- 1¾ cups water
- 1½ cups peeled and seeded winter squash cut into ½-inch pieces
- 1 14.5-ounce can Mexican-style stewed tomatoes, undrained, cut up
- 2 cups chopped cooked chicken or turkey (10 ounces)
- 1 cup loose-pack frozen whole kernel corn
- ¼ cup snipped fresh cilantro (optional)

1 In a 4-quart Dutch oven, heat oil over medium heat. Add onion and sweet pepper; cook for about 5 minutes or until tender, stirring occasionally. Stir in chili powder and cumin; cook and stir for 30 seconds.

2 Add chicken broth, water, squash, and tomatoes. Bring to boiling; reduce heat. Cover and simmer for about 20 minutes or until squash is tender, stirring occasionally. Stir in chicken and corn. Heat through. If desired, sprinkle with cilantro.

Nutrition facts per serving: 180 cal., 4 g total fat (1 g sat. fat), 40 mg chol., 594 mg sodium, 19 g carb., 2 g dietary fiber, 19 g protein.

spinach, CHICKEN, AND WILD RICE SOUP

Prep: 15 minutes
Cook: 7 to 8 hours (low)
or 3½ to 4 hours
(high)
Makes: 6 servings

3   **cups water**

1   **14-ounce can chicken
    broth**

1   **10.75-ounce can
    condensed cream of
    chicken soup**

⅔   **cup wild rice, rinsed
    and drained**

½   **teaspoon dried thyme,
    crushed**

¼   **teaspoon ground black
    pepper**

3   **cups chopped cooked
    chicken or turkey
    (15 ounces)**

2   **cups shredded fresh
    spinach**

1 In a 3½- or 4-quart slow cooker, combine water, broth, soup, wild rice, thyme, and pepper.

2 Cover and cook on low-heat setting for 7 to 8 hours or on high-heat setting for 3½ to 4 hours. Stir in chicken and spinach.

Nutrition facts per serving: 263 cal., 9 g total fat (3 g sat. fat), 66 mg chol., 741 mg sodium, 19 g carb., 2 g dietary fiber, 25 g protein.

kale, LENTIL, AND CHICKEN SOUP

Prep: 25 minutes
Cook: 20 minutes
Makes: 6 servings

- 1 tablespoon olive oil
- 1 cup chopped onion
- 1 cup coarsely chopped carrots
- 2 cloves garlic, minced
- 6 cups reduced-sodium chicken broth
- 1 tablespoon snipped fresh basil, or 1 teaspoon dried basil, crushed
- 4 cups coarsely chopped kale (about 8 ounces)
- ½ teaspoon salt
- ⅛ teaspoon ground black pepper
- 1½ cups cubed cooked chicken (about 8 ounces)
- 1 medium tomato, seeded and chopped
- ½ cup dried red lentils*

1 In a large saucepan, heat oil over medium-low heat. Add onion, carrots, and garlic. Cover and cook for 5 to 7 minutes or until vegetables are nearly tender, stirring occasionally.

2 Add broth and dried basil (if using) to vegetable mixture. Bring to boiling; reduce heat. Cover and simmer for 10 minutes. Stir in kale, salt, and pepper. Return to boiling; reduce heat. Cover and simmer for 10 minutes.

3 Stir in chicken, tomato, red lentils, and fresh basil (if using). Cover and simmer for 5 to 10 minutes more or until kale and lentils are tender.

Nutrition facts per serving: 199 cal., 5 g total fat (1 g sat. fat), 31 mg chol., 833 mg sodium, 20 g carb., 5 g dietary fiber, 18 g protein.

*Tip: If you wish to substitute brown or yellow lentils for the red lentils, you'll need to increase the cooking time. Check package directions for cooking times and add the lentils in Step 2.

choose-a-vegetable
CHICKEN AND PASTA SOUP

Start to Finish: 40 minutes
Makes: 6 servings

2　**14-ounce cans reduced-sodium chicken broth**

2　**cups water**

1　**tablespoon snipped fresh basil, or 1 teaspoon dried basil, crushed**

¼　**teaspoon ground black pepper**

1　**cup dried multigrain or regular elbow macaroni**

3　**cups vegetables, such as thinly sliced carrots, packaged broccoli florets, and/or chopped green or red sweet pepper**

1½　**cups cubed cooked chicken breast (about 8 ounces)**

¼　**cup finely shredded Parmesan cheese (1 ounce)**

In a Dutch oven, combine broth, water, dried basil (if using), and black pepper; bring to boiling. Stir in pasta. Return to boiling; reduce heat. Simmer, covered, for 5 minutes. Stir in vegetables. Return to boiling; reduce heat. Simmer, covered, for 5 to 8 minutes more or until vegetables and pasta are tender. Stir in chicken; heat through. To serve, stir in fresh basil (if using) and top with Parmesan cheese.

Nutrition facts per serving: 161 cal., 3 g total fat (1 g sat. fat), 34 mg chol., 420 mg sodium, 16 g carb., 3 g dietary fiber, 18 g protein.

chicken PAPRIKASH SOUP

This Hungarian-style soup would be delicious ladled over hot cooked spaetzle or egg noodles.

Prep: 10 minutes
Cook: 15 minutes
Makes: 6 servings

¼ cup all-purpose flour

2 tablespoons paprika

½ teaspoon salt

¼ teaspoon ground black pepper

1½ pounds chicken breast tenderloins, cut in half

2 14-ounce cans chicken broth

1 tablespoon vegetable oil

1 cup frozen chopped onion, thawed and drained

2 teaspoons bottled minced garlic

½ of a 2-ounce package refrigerated sliced potatoes

6 tablespoons sour cream

1 In a resealable plastic bag, combine flour, paprika, salt, and pepper. Add half of the chicken; shake to coat. Place coated chicken on a plate and set aside. Repeat with remaining chicken.

2 In a small bowl, stir together flour mixture remaining in the plastic bag and 3 tablespoons of the chicken broth.

3 In a large saucepan, heat oil over medium-high heat. Add chicken; cook for about 4 minutes or until browned. Add onion and garlic; cook for 1 minute. Stir in the remaining chicken broth and potatoes. Bring to boiling; reduce heat. Simmer, covered, for 5 minutes.

4 Stir in flour mixture. Cook and stir until thickened and bubbly. Cook and stir for 1 minute more.

5 Ladle soup into bowls; top with sour cream.

Nutrition facts per serving: 262 cal., 11 g total fat (4 g sat. fat), 72 mg chol., 821 mg sodium, 16 g carb., 2 g dietary fiber, 26 g protein.

creamed CHICKEN AND CORN SOUP

Prep: 20 minutes
Cook: 5 to 6 hours (low) or 2½ to 3 hours (high)
Makes: 4 to 6 servings

12 ounces skinless, boneless chicken thighs

1 26-ounce can condensed cream of chicken soup

1 14.75-ounce can cream-style corn

1 14-ounce can reduced-sodium chicken broth

1 cup chopped carrots (2 medium)

1 cup finely chopped onion (1 large)

1 cup frozen whole kernel corn

½ cup chopped celery (1 stalk)

½ cup water

2 slices bacon, crisp-cooked, drained, and crumbled

1 In a 3½- or 4-quart slow cooker, combine chicken, soup, cream-style corn, broth, carrots, onion, frozen corn, celery, and the water.

2 Cover and cook on low-heat setting for 5 to 6 hours or on high-heat setting for 2½ to 3 hours.

3 Remove chicken from cooker; cool slightly. Chop chicken; stir back into soup mixture. Sprinkle each serving with bacon.

Nutrition facts per serving: 447 cal., 17 g total fat (5 g sat. fat), 90 mg chol., 2056 mg sodium, 50 g carb., 5 g dietary fiber, 28 g protein.

chicken-and-apple
CURRY SOUP

Prep: 25 minutes
Cook: 6 to 7 hours (low)
       or 3 to 3½ hours
       (high)
Makes: 6 servings

1½ **cups chopped, unpeeled
    apple (1 large)**

1   **cup chopped celery
    (2 stalks)**

1   **cup chopped carrots
    (2 medium)**

½   **cup chopped onion
    (1 medium)**

2   **14-ounce cans chicken
    broth**

1   **cup apple juice**

2   **tablespoons quick-
    cooking tapioca, crushed**

2   **teaspoons curry powder**

½   **teaspoon salt**

½   **teaspoon dried thyme,
    crushed**

1   **pound cooked, cubed
    chicken breast**

½   **cup half-and-half or
    light cream**

2   **cups hot cooked rice**

    **Thinly sliced apple
    (optional)**

    **Fresh thyme sprigs
    (optional)**

1 In a 3½- or 4-quart slow cooker, combine apple, celery, carrots, and onion. Stir broth, apple juice, tapioca, curry powder, salt, and thyme into mixture in cooker.

2 Cover and cook on low-heat setting for 6 to 7 hours or on high-heat setting for 3 to 3½ hours.

3 Just before serving, stir chicken and half-and-half into cooker. If using low-heat setting, turn to high-heat setting. Cover and cook for 10 minutes or until heated through. Serve with hot cooked rice. If desired, garnish individual servings with apple slices and thyme sprigs.

Nutrition facts per serving: 293 cal., 6 g total fat (2 g sat. fat), 73 mg chol., 817 mg sodium, 32 g carb., 2 g dietary fiber, 27 g protein.

in-a-hurry CHICKEN CURRY

Frozen stew vegetables eliminate peeling and cutting, which keeps prep time to a quick 15 minutes.

Prep: 15 minutes
Cook: 6 to 7 hours (low)
or 3 to 3½ hours
(high)
Makes: 6 servings

1 **16-ounce package frozen stew vegetables**

4 **large chicken thighs, skin removed (1½ to 1¾ pounds)**

¼ **teaspoon ground black pepper**

1 **10.75-ounce can reduced-fat and reduced-sodium condensed cream of chicken soup**

2 **teaspoons curry powder**

1 **tablespoon snipped fresh cilantro**

1 Place frozen stew vegetables in a 3½- or 4-quart slow cooker. Top with chicken. Sprinkle with pepper. In a small bowl, stir together soup and curry powder. Pour soup mixture over all.

2 Cover and cook on low-heat setting for 6 to 7 hours or on high-heat setting for 3 to 3½ hours. Remove chicken from bones and, if desired, break into large pieces. Sprinkle with cilantro.

Nutrition facts per serving: 199 cal., 6 g total fat (2 g sat. fat), 98 mg chol., 320 mg sodium, 13 g carb., 1 g dietary fiber, 24 g protein.

chicken AND SAUSAGE GUMBO

Prep: 25 minutes
Cook: 6 to 7 hours (low)
or 3 to 3½ hours
(high)
Makes: 8 servings

⅓ **cup all-purpose flour**

1 **14-ounce can reduced-sodium chicken broth**

2 **cups chopped cooked chicken breast or turkey breast (10 ounces)**

8 **ounces smoked turkey sausage links, quartered lengthwise and sliced**

2 **cups sliced fresh okra or one 10-ounce package frozen cut okra, partially thawed**

1 **cup water**

1 **cup coarsely chopped onion (1 large)**

1 **cup coarsely chopped red or green sweet pepper (1 large)**

½ **cup sliced celery (1 stalk)**

4 **cloves garlic, minced**

1 **teaspoon dried thyme, crushed**

½ **teaspoon black ground pepper**

¼ **teaspoon cayenne pepper**

3 **cups hot cooked brown rice**

① For roux, in a heavy medium saucepan cook flour over medium heat for about 6 minutes or until brown, stirring occasionally. Remove from heat; cool slightly. Gradually stir broth into flour. Cook and stir over medium heat until thickened and bubbly.

② Pour flour mixture into a 3½- or 4-quart slow cooker. Add chicken, sausage, okra, the water, onion, sweet pepper, celery, garlic, thyme, black pepper, and cayenne.

③ Cover and cook on low-heat setting for 6 to 7 hours or on high-heat setting for 3 to 3½ hours. Skim off fat. Serve gumbo over hot cooked brown rice.

Nutrition facts per serving: 230 cal., 5 g total fat (1 g sat. fat), 48 mg chol., 425 mg sodium, 27 g carb., 3 g dietary fiber, 19 g protein.

chicken stew WITH POTATO DUMPLINGS

Prep: 30 minutes
Cook: 6 hours (low) or
      4 hours (high)
Makes: 8 servings

- **3 pounds bone-in chicken thighs, skin removed**
- **2 large carrots, peeled and cut into ½-inch-thick slices**
- **2 stalks celery, cut into ½-inch pieces**
- **3 medium parsnips, peeled and cut into ½-inch-thick slices**
- **1 large sweet potato (about 1 pound), peeled and cut into 1-inch cubes**
- **4 scallions, trimmed and chopped**
- **4 cups chicken broth**
- **1 cup water**
- **½ teaspoon dried sage leaves**
- **¼ teaspoon salt**
- **¼ teaspoon ground black pepper**
- **1 package shelf-stable, fully cooked gnocchi (dumplings)**
- **2 tablespoons cornstarch mixed with ¼ cup cold water**
- **Hot pepper sauce**

1 Place chicken in 6-quart slow cooker. Top with carrots, celery, parsnips, sweet potato, and scallions. Pour chicken broth and the water over. Sprinkle with sage, salt, and pepper.

2 Cover and cook on low-heat setting for 6 hours or on high-heat setting for 4 hours.

3 Transfer chicken to a cutting board. If necessary, raise temperature to high-heat setting. Add gnocchi to mixture in slow cooker. Cover slow cooker; cook for 10 minutes. Meanwhile, let chicken cool slightly. Using two forks, remove chicken from bones and pull chicken apart into shreds; discard bones.

4 When gnocchi are cooked, return chicken to slow cooker. Stir cornstarch mixture and add to slow cooker. Cover slow cooker; cook for 10 to 20 minutes or until thickened slightly. Add hot pepper sauce to taste before serving.

Nutrition facts per serving: 362 cal., 10 g total fat (3 g sat. fat), 72 mg chol., 881 mg sodium, 45 g carb., 4 g dietary fiber, 23 g protein.

chicken stew WITH TORTELLINI

Dress up leftover chicken by stirring it into this easy-to-prepare stew. Chunks of yellow squash and sweet pepper accompany plump tortellini and spinach.

Start to Finish: 35 minutes
Makes: 6 servings

1½ **cups water**

2 **14-ounce cans reduced-sodium chicken broth**

1 **medium yellow summer squash**

1 **green sweet pepper, coarsely chopped**

1 **cup dried cheese-filled tortellini**

2 **medium carrots, sliced**

1 **medium onion, cut into thin wedges**

¼ **teaspoon garlic-pepper seasoning**

2½ **cups chopped cooked chicken breast (13 ounces)**

2 **cups torn fresh spinach**

2 **tablespoons snipped fresh basil**

1 In a Dutch oven, bring water and chicken broth to boiling. Meanwhile, halve summer squash lengthwise and cut into ½-inch slices. Add squash, sweet pepper, pasta, carrot, onion, and garlic-pepper to Dutch oven.

2 Return to boiling; reduce heat. Simmer, covered, for about 15 minutes or until pasta and vegetables are nearly tender.

3 Stir in chicken. Cook, covered, for 5 minutes more or until pasta, carrots, and onion are tender. Stir spinach and fresh basil into soup.

Nutrition facts per serving: 206 cal., 4 g total fat (1 g sat. fat), 50 mg chol., 561 mg sodium, 17 g carb., 2 g dietary fiber, 25 g protein.

spanish CHICKEN STEW

Though olives may not be the first condiment most cooks would think of to season a stew, they give grand flavor to this Spanish-inspired chicken dish.

Prep: 15 minutes
Cook: 20 minutes
Makes: 4 servings

1¼ **pounds skinless, boneless chicken thighs, cut into 1½-inch pieces**

¼ **teaspoon salt**

¼ **teaspoon ground black pepper**

1 **tablespoon olive oil**

1 **medium onion, thinly sliced**

1 **red sweet pepper, cut into ¼-inch strips**

2 **cloves garlic, minced**

1 **cup chicken broth**

12 **ounces red potatoes, cut into ½-inch wedges**

½ **teaspoon dried savory, crushed**

¼ **teaspoon dried thyme, crushed**

1 **14.5-ounce can diced tomatoes, undrained**

⅓ **cup small pimiento-stuffed olives, cut up**

① Season chicken with salt and pepper. In a large Dutch oven, cook chicken in hot oil over medium-high heat until light brown.

② Add onion and sweet pepper to Dutch oven; cook for about 3 minutes or until crisp-tender. Add garlic; cook for 30 seconds more. Add broth, potato wedges, savory, and thyme. Bring to boiling; reduce heat. Simmer, covered, for about 15 minutes or until chicken and potatoes are tender. Stir in tomatoes. Return to boiling; reduce heat. Simmer, covered, for 5 minutes. Remove from heat. Stir in olives.

Nutrition facts per serving: 334 cal., 11 g total fat (2 g sat. fat), 113 mg chol., 918 mg sodium, 24 g carb., 3 g dietary fiber, 32 g protein.

coq au vin STEW

Beefy onion soup mix and red wine combine with chicken for a stew that's luscious and comforting on a cold night.

Prep: 20 minutes
Cook: 5 to 6 hours (low)
    or 2½ to 3 hours
    (high)
Makes: 6 servings

3 pounds chicken thighs,
   skinned

1 envelope (½ of a
   2.2-ounce package)
   beefy onion soup mix

2 cups quartered fresh
   mushrooms

1½ cups frozen small whole
    onions

3 medium carrots, cut into
   3½-inch sticks

½ cup dry red wine

2 cups hot cooked mashed
   potatoes

   Snipped fresh parsley

1 Lightly coat a large skillet with cooking spray. Heat skillet over medium heat. Cook chicken thighs, several at a time, in the hot skillet until brown. Drain off fat.

2 Place chicken thighs in a 3½- or 4-quart slow cooker. Sprinkle chicken thighs with dry soup mix. Add mushrooms, onions, and carrots. Pour wine over all in cooker.

3 Cover and cook on low-heat setting for 5 to 6 hours or on high-heat setting for 2½ to 3 hours. Serve with mashed potatoes and sprinkle with parsley.

Nutrition facts per serving: 269 cal., 6 g total fat (1 g sat. fat), 107 mg chol., 627 mg sodium, 20 g carb., 2 g dietary fiber, 29 g protein.

nacho CHEESE CHICKEN CHOWDER

Prep: 10 minutes
Cook: 4 hours to 5 hours
(low) or 2 to
2½ hours (high)
Makes: 6 servings

1 **pound skinless, boneless chicken breast halves, cut into ½-inch pieces**

2 **14.5-ounce cans Mexican-style stewed tomatoes, undrained**

1 **10.75-ounce can condensed nacho cheese soup**

1 **10-ounce package frozen whole kernel corn, thawed**

Shredded Mexican-blend or cheddar cheese

1 In a 3½- or 4-quart slow cooker, combine chicken, tomatoes, soup, and corn.

2 Cover and cook on low-heat setting for 4 to 5 hours or on high-heat setting for 2 to 2½ hours. Sprinkle each serving with cheese.

Nutrition facts per serving: 244 cal., 6 g total fat (3 g sat. fat), 55 mg chol., 347 mg sodium, 24 g carb., 2 g dietary fiber, 23 g protein.

turkey AND MUSHROOM SOUP

If possible, seek out the less common varieties of mushrooms, such as the meaty shiitake or the earthly porcini. They'll add an exotic richness to this soup.

Start to Finish: 35 minutes
Makes: 4 servings

- 2 **cups sliced fresh mushrooms (such as cremini, shiitake, porcini, or button)**
- ½ **cup thinly sliced celery (1 stalk)**
- ½ **cup thinly sliced carrot (1 medium)**
- ⅓ **cup chopped onion (1 small)**
- 1 **tablespoon butter or margarine**
- 4½ **cups water**
- 1 **tablespoon instant chicken bouillon granules**
- ⅛ **teaspoon ground black pepper**
- ½ **cup dried orzo**
- 1½ **cups chopped cooked turkey (8 ounces)**
- 2 **tablespoons snipped fresh parsley**
- 1 **teaspoon snipped fresh thyme**

1 In a large saucepan, cook mushrooms, celery, carrot, and onion in hot butter until crisp-tender. Add water, bouillon granules, and pepper.

2 Bring to boiling; stir in orzo. Return to boiling; reduce heat. Simmer, uncovered, for 5 to 8 minutes or until orzo is tender but still firm. Stir in turkey, parsley, and thyme; heat through.

Nutrition facts per serving: 199 cal., 6 g total fat (2 g sat. fat), 40 mg chol., 767 mg sodium, 17 g carb., 2 g dietary fiber, 19 g protein.

yucatan-style TURKEY AND VEGETABLE SOUP

Queso fresco is a mild Mexican cheese with a crumbly texture similar to that of feta or farmer's cheese. Look for it at Hispanic food markets or larger supermarkets.

Prep: 35 minutes
Cook: 15 minutes
Makes: 6 servings

1 medium onion, thinly sliced

3 or 4 cloves garlic

1 tablespoon cooking oil

2 canned chipotle chile peppers in adobo sauce, drained and chopped*

2 medium carrots, chopped

5 cups reduced-sodium chicken broth or turkey stock

2 cups coarsely chopped tomatoes

⅛ teaspoon salt

1 pound cooked turkey, cubed or shredded (about 3 cups)

2 small zucchini, chopped (2 cups)

2 tablespoons snipped fresh cilantro

⅓ cup crumbled queso fresco or feta cheese

1 avocado, pitted, peeled, and chopped

Thin strips fresh lime peel (optional)

1 lime, cut into wedges (optional)

1 In a dry medium skillet, combine onion slices and unpeeled garlic cloves; cook and stir for 3 to 5 minutes or until edges are brown. Chop onion; peel and slice garlic cloves.

2 In a 4-quart Dutch oven, heat oil over medium-high heat. Add chopped onion, sliced garlic, and chipotle peppers. Cook and stir for 3 minutes. Add carrots. Cook and stir for 3 minutes more.

3 Add broth, tomatoes, and salt. Bring to boiling; reduce heat. Cover and simmer for 10 minutes. Add turkey, zucchini, and cilantro; cover and cook for 5 minutes more.

4 Top with queso fresco, avocado and (if desired) lime peel strips. Serve with lime wedges, if desired.

Nutrition facts per serving: 229 cal., 8 g total fat (2 g sat. fat), 65 mg chol., 609 mg sodium, 12 g carb., 4 g dietary fiber, 27 g protein.

*Tip: Because chile peppers contain volatile oils that can burn your skin and eyes, avoid direct contact with them as much as possible. When working with chile peppers, wear plastic or rubber gloves. If your bare hands do touch the peppers, wash your hands and nails well with soap and warm water.

turkey AND TORTILLA SOUP

Start to Finish: 20 minutes
Makes: 4 servings

3 6-inch corn tortillas, cut
    into strips

2 tablespoons vegetable oil

2 14-ounce cans reduced-
    sodium chicken broth

1 cup red or green salsa

2 cups cubed cooked turkey
    or chicken

1 large zucchini, coarsely
    chopped (1½ cups)

   Lime wedges (optional)

   Sour cream (optional)

   Snipped fresh cilantro
    (optional)

1 In a large skillet, cook tortilla strips in hot oil until crisp. Use a slotted spoon to remove from skillet; drain on paper towels.

2 In a large saucepan, combine broth and salsa. Bring to boiling over medium-high heat. Stir in turkey and zucchini; heat through.

3 Serve with tortilla strips. If desired, top each serving with lime wedges, sour cream, and cilantro.

Nutrition facts per serving: 262 cal., 11 g total fat (2 g sat. fat), 53 mg chol., 920 mg sodium, 16 g carb., 3 g dietary fiber, 26 g protein.

turkey FRAME SOUP

Prep: 30 minutes
Cook: 1¾ hours
Makes: 6 servings

1 **meaty turkey frame**

4 **cups water**

4 **cups turkey or chicken broth**

1 **large onion, quartered**

1 **clove garlic, crushed**

½ **teaspoon salt**

¼ **cup sun-dried tomatoes, cut into thin strips**

1½ **teaspoons dried Italian seasoning**

¼ **teaspoon ground black pepper**

3 **cups sliced or cubed vegetables, such as carrots, parsnips, or turnips**

1½ **cups high-fiber or whole wheat pasta, such as rotini or penne**

1 **15-ounce can Great Northern beans or white kidney beans, rinsed and drained**

Grated Parmesan cheese (optional)

① Break turkey frame or cut in half with kitchen shears. Place in a large pot. Add the water, broth, onion, garlic, and salt. Bring to boiling; reduce heat. Cover and simmer for 1½ hours.

② Remove turkey frame. Cool; remove meat from bones; coarsely chop meat. Measure enough turkey to equal 2 cups. Discard bones. Strain broth; skim off fat.

③ Return broth to pot. Stir in tomatoes, Italian seasoning, and pepper. Stir in vegetables. Return to boiling; reduce heat. Simmer, covered, for 5 minutes. Add pasta. Simmer, uncovered, for 8 to 10 minutes or until pasta is tender and still firm and vegetables are tender. Stir in turkey and beans; heat through. Serve with grated Parmesan cheese.

Nutrition facts per serving: 303 cal., 4 g total fat (1 g sat. fat), 37 mg chol., 965 mg sodium, 42 g carb., 8 g dietary fiber, 26 g protein.

asian TURKEY AND RICE SOUP

Prep: 25 minutes
Cook: 7 to 8 hours (low)
or 3½ to 4 hours
(high)
Makes: 6 servings

1 **pound turkey breast
tenderloin or skinless,
boneless chicken breast
halves, cut into
1-inch pieces**

2 **cups sliced fresh
mushrooms (such as
shiitake or button)**

1 **cup carrots cut into thin
bite-size strips
(2 medium)**

½ **cup chopped onion
(1 medium)**

2 **14-ounce cans reduced-
sodium chicken broth**

1½ **cups water**

2 **tablespoons reduced-
sodium soy sauce**

2 **teaspoons minced fresh
ginger**

2 **teaspoons minced garlic**

1½ **cups sliced bok choy**

1 **cup instant brown rice
Chow mein noodles
(optional)**

① In a 3½- or 4-quart slow cooker, combine turkey, mushrooms, carrots, and onion. Pour broth and the water over turkey and vegetables. Stir in soy sauce, ginger, and garlic.

② Cover and cook on low-heat setting for 7 to 8 hours or on high-heat setting for 3½ to 4 hours.

③ If using low-heat setting, turn to high-heat setting. Stir bok choy and rice into turkey mixture. Cover and cook for 10 to 15 minutes more or until rice is tender. If desired, top each serving with chow mein noodles.

Nutrition facts per serving: 166 cal., 2 g total fat (0 g sat. fat), 45 mg chol., 572 mg sodium, 15 g carb., 2 g dietary fiber, 22 g protein.

golden TURKEY–SPLIT PEA SOUP

Yellow split peas add an autumnal hue. During cooking, the peas soften and begin to fall apart, which helps bring a pleasing—but not overly thick—consistency to this delicious soup.

Prep: 20 minutes
Cook: 9 to 10 hours (low)
      or 4½ to 5 hours
      (high)
Makes: 6 servings

2 **cups dried yellow
   split peas**

2 **14-ounce cans reduced-
   sodium chicken broth**

2 **cups water**

2 **cups frozen whole kernel
   corn**

1½ **cups sliced carrots
   (3 medium)**

1 **10.75-ounce can
   condensed cream of
   chicken soup**

8 **ounces cooked smoked
   turkey sausage, halved
   lengthwise and sliced**

½ **cup sliced scallions (4)**

½ **cup chopped red sweet
   pepper (1 medium)**

2 **teaspoons dried thyme,
   crushed**

① Rinse and drain split peas. In a 4½- or 5-quart slow cooker, combine split peas, broth, water, frozen corn, carrots, soup, turkey sausage, scallions, sweet pepper, and thyme.

② Cover and cook on low-heat setting for 9 to 10 hours or on high-heat setting for 4½ to 5 hours.

Nutrition facts per serving: 409 cal., 8 g total fat (2 g sat. fat), 30 mg chol., 1076 mg sodium, 60 g carb., 19 g dietary fiber, 27 g protein.

turkey AND SWEET POTATO CHOWDER

This recipe is a terrific way to use leftover turkey. But if you don't have leftovers, buy a cooked turkey breast half or substitute chopped cooked chicken.

Prep: 15 minutes
Cook: 24 minutes
Makes: 5 servings

1 large potato, peeled, if desired, and chopped (about 1½ cups)

1 14-ounce can reduced-sodium chicken broth

2 small ears frozen corn on the cob, thawed, or 1 cup loose-pack frozen whole kernel corn

1 medium sweet potato, peeled and cut into ¾-inch cubes (about 1½ cups)

1 teaspoon snipped fresh thyme, or ¼ teaspoon dried thyme, crushed

⅛ to ¼ teaspoon ground black pepper

12 ounces cooked turkey breast, cut into ½-inch cubes (about 2¼ cups)

1½ cups fat-free milk

1 In a 3-quart saucepan, combine chopped potato and broth. Bring to boiling; reduce heat. Simmer, uncovered, for about 12 minutes or until potato is tender, stirring occasionally. Remove from heat. Do not drain. Using a potato masher, mash potato until mixture is thickened and nearly smooth.

2 If using corn on the cob, carefully cut crosswise into ½-inch-thick slices.

3 Stir corn pieces or frozen corn kernels, sweet potato, dried thyme (if using), and pepper into potato mixture in saucepan. Bring to boiling; reduce heat. Cover and cook for 12 to 15 minutes or until the sweet potato is tender. Stir in turkey and milk; heat through.

4 To serve, ladle chowder into bowls. Sprinkle with fresh thyme (if using).

Nutrition facts per serving: 229 cal., 1 g total fat (0 g sat. fat), 58 mg chol., 279 mg sodium, 29 g carb., 2 g dietary fiber, 27 g protein.

turkey-corn CHOWDER

Start to Finish: 35 minutes
Makes: 4 servings

- 1 **14-ounce can chicken broth**
- 1 **large russet potato, peeled and chopped (about 1½ cups)**
- 2 **small ears frozen corn on the cob, thawed**
- 12 **ounces cooked turkey breast, cut into ½-inch cubes (about 2½ cups)**
- 1 **large sweet potato, peeled and cut into ¾-inch cubes (about 1½ cups)**
- 1½ **cups milk**
- ¼ **teaspoon ground black pepper**
- ¼ **cup snipped fresh parsley**

1. In a large saucepan, combine chicken broth and russet potato. Bring just to boiling; reduce heat. Simmer, uncovered, for about 12 minutes or until potato is tender, stirring occasionally. Remove from heat. Using a potato masher, mash potato until mixture is thickened and smooth.

2. Cut off kernels from one ear of corn; cut second ear crosswise into ½-inch-thick pieces. Stir corn, turkey, sweet potato, milk, and pepper into potato mixture.

3. Bring to boiling; reduce heat. Cook, uncovered, for 12 to 15 minutes or until sweet potato is tender. Sprinkle each serving with parsley.

Nutrition facts per serving: 309 cal., 5 g total fat (2 g sat. fat), 66 mg chol., 381 mg sodium, 32 g carb., 4 g dietary fiber, 33 g protein.

Make-Ahead Directions: Peel and cut up the potatoes, turkey, and parsley the day before. Refrigerate the potatoes, covered, in water. Refrigerate the turkey and parsley separately in airtight containers.

beef,
PORK, AND LAMB

Barley-Beef Soup, *page 60*

all-american
CHEESEBURGER SOUP

Start to Finish: 40 minutes
Makes: 6 servings

1 **pound ground beef**

1 **medium onion, chopped**

1 **stalk celery, chopped**

2 **cloves garlic, minced**

2 **tablespoons all-purpose flour**

2 **14-ounce cans reduced-sodium beef broth**

2 **medium potatoes, scrubbed and coarsely chopped**

1 **14.5-ounce can diced tomatoes, drained**

1 **8-ounce package shredded cheddar and American cheese blend (2 cups)**

1 **6-ounce can tomato paste**

¼ **cup ketchup**

2 **tablespoons Dijon-style mustard**

1 **cup whole milk**

Broiled or toasted buns or rolls*

Cheeseburger toppings, such as pickles, onions, lettuce, mustard, and/or ketchup (optional)

1 In 4-quart Dutch oven, cook beef, onion, celery, and garlic over medium heat until meat is browned and vegetables are tender; drain off fat. Sprinkle flour on beef mixture; cook and stir for 2 minutes. Stir in broth and potatoes. Bring to boiling, stirring occasionally. Reduce heat. Simmer, covered, for 10 minutes or until potatoes are tender.

2 Stir in tomatoes, cheese, tomato paste, ketchup, and mustard. Cook and stir until cheese is melted and smooth and soup just comes to a gentle boil. Stir in milk; heat through. Serve with toasted bun halves and cheeseburger toppings.

*Broiled Buns: Split 3 cocktail buns or brown-and-serve rolls and place, cut side up, on a broiler pan. Brush lightly with 1 tablespoon melted butter or olive oil. Broil 3 to 4 inches from heat for about 1 minute or until lightly toasted. Or, using a grill pan, brush buns as above and grill buns, cut sides down, over medium-high heat for 1 to 2 minutes or until toasted.

Nutrition facts per serving: 477 cal., 27 g total fat (13 g sat. fat), 93 mg chol., 1309 mg sodium, 28 g carb., 4 g dietary fiber, 29 g protein.

kansas CITY STEAK SOUP

Prep: 15 minutes
Cook: 25 minutes
Makes: 6 servings

1½ pounds lean ground beef
    (sirloin)

1 cup chopped onion
    (1 large)

1 cup sliced celery (2 stalks)

2 14-ounce cans reduced-
    sodium beef broth or
    3½ cups beef stock

1 28-ounce can diced
    tomatoes, undrained

1 10-ounce package frozen
    mixed vegetables

2 tablespoons steak sauce

2 teaspoons Worcestershire
    sauce

¼ teaspoon salt

¼ teaspoon ground black
    pepper

¼ cup all-purpose flour

1 In a large pot, cook beef, onion, and celery over medium heat until meat is brown and vegetables are tender. Drain well; return to pot.

2 Stir in 1 can of the beef broth, the tomatoes, mixed vegetables, steak sauce, Worcestershire sauce, salt, and pepper. Bring to boiling; reduce heat. Simmer, covered, for 20 minutes.

3 In a medium bowl, whisk together remaining can of beef broth and the flour. Stir into mixture in pot. Cook until thickened and bubbly. Cook and stir 1 minute more.

Nutrition facts per serving: 306 cal., 12 g total fat (5 g sat. fat), 74 mg chol., 747 mg sodium, 21 g carb., 4 g dietary fiber, 27 g protein.

mediterranean
MEATBALL SOUP

Prep: 25 minutes
Bake: 15 minutes
Cook: 20 minutes
Oven: 350°F
Makes: 6 servings

¾ **cup soft whole wheat bread crumbs**

1 **egg, lightly beaten**

4 **cloves garlic, minced**

2 **teaspoons snipped fresh rosemary, or ½ teaspoon dried rosemary, crushed**

¼ **teaspoon ground black pepper**

1 **pound 90% or higher lean ground beef**

1 **tablespoon olive oil**

3 **medium carrots, peeled and coarsely chopped**

2 **medium yellow and/or red sweet peppers, seeded and cut into bite-size strips**

1 **medium onion, chopped**

2 **cups reduced-sodium beef stock**

2 **cups water**

1 **15-ounce can Great Northern beans, rinsed and drained**

½ **cup quick-cooking barley**

4 **cups baby spinach leaves**

1 Preheat oven to 350°F. In a large bowl, combine bread crumbs, egg, half of the garlic, half of the rosemary, and the black pepper. Add ground beef; mix well. Shape meat mixture into 1½-inch meatballs. Place meatballs in a foil-lined 15x10x1-inch baking pan. Bake for about 15 minutes or until done in centers (160°F). Set aside.

2 In a 5- to 6-quart Dutch oven, heat oil over medium heat. Add carrots, sweet peppers, onion, and the remaining garlic; cook for 5 minutes, stirring occasionally. Add beef stock, the water, Great Northern beans, barley, and the remaining rosemary. Bring to boiling; reduce heat. Cover and simmer for about 15 minutes or until barley is tender.

3 Add meatballs to barley mixture; heat through. Stir in spinach just before serving.

Nutrition facts per serving: 301 cal., 10 g total fat (3 g sat. fat), 49 mg chol., 400 mg sodium, 31 g carb., 7 g dietary fiber, 25 g protein.

busy-day BEEF-VEGETABLE SOUP

Prep: 20 minutes
Cook: 8 to 10 hours (low)
or 4 to 5 hours
(high)
Makes: 4 servings

1 pound boneless beef
chuck pot roast

3 medium carrots, peeled
and cut into ½-inch pieces

2 small potatoes, cut into
½-inch pieces

½ cup chopped onion
(1 medium)

½ teaspoon salt

½ teaspoon dried thyme,
crushed

1 bay leaf

2 14.5-ounce cans diced
tomatoes, undrained

1 cup water

½ cup frozen peas

Fresh parsley sprigs
(optional)

1 Trim fat from meat. Cut meat into ¾-inch pieces. In 3½- or 4-quart slow cooker, combine meat, carrots, potatoes, and onion. Sprinkle with salt and thyme; add bay leaf. Pour tomatoes and the water over contents.

2 Cover and cook on low-heat setting for 8 to 10 hours or on high-heat setting for 4 to 5 hours. Discard bay leaf. Stir in frozen peas. If desired, garnish each serving with parsley.

Nutrition facts per serving: 269 cal., 4 g total fat (1 g sat. fat), 67 mg chol., 746 mg sodium, 29 g carb., 4 g dietary fiber, 28 g protein.

french onion AND BEEF SOUP

Start to Finish: 20 minutes
Oven: Broil
Makes: 4 servings

- 3 **tablespoons butter**
- 1 **medium onion, thinly sliced and separated into rings**
- 2 **10.5-ounce cans condensed French onion soup**
- 2½ **cups water**
- 2 **cups cubed cooked roast beef**
- 4 **1-inch slices French bread**
- ½ **cup shredded Gruyère or Swiss cheese (2 ounces)**

1 Preheat broiler. In a large skillet, heat butter over medium heat. Add onion; cook for about 5 minutes or until very tender. Stir in soup, water, and beef. Bring to boiling, stirring occasionally.

2 Meanwhile, place bread slices on a baking sheet. Broil about 4 inches from the heat for about 1 minute or until toasted on one side. Sprinkle toasted sides with cheese. Broil for about 1 minute more or until cheese is melted.

3 Serve soup with toasted cheese bread.

Nutrition facts per serving: 465 cal., 21 g total fat (10 g sat. fat), 82 mg chol., 1701 mg sodium, 40 g carb., 3 g dietary fiber, 28 g protein.

beef AND VEGETABLE SOUP WITH PASTA

Prep: 20 minutes
Cook: 10 minutes
Makes: 6 to 8 servings

1 **17-ounce package refrigerated cooked beef tips with gravy**

3 **14-ounce cans beef broth**

1 **15- to 16-ounce can Great Northern beans or cannellini beans, rinsed and drained**

1 **14.5-ounce can diced tomatoes with garlic, basil, and oregano**

1 **10-ounce package frozen mixed vegetables**

1 **cup dried small pasta (such as macaroni, small shells, mini penne, or rotini)**

Crusty bread (optional)

Shredded Parmesan cheese (optional)

In a 4-quart Dutch oven, stir together beef tips and gravy, broth, beans, undrained tomatoes, and vegetables. Bring to boiling. Stir in pasta. Return to boiling; reduce heat. Simmer, uncovered, for about 10 minutes, or until pasta is tender. If desired, serve with bread and sprinkle each serving with Parmesan cheese.

Nutrition facts per serving: 319 cal., 5 g total fat (2 g sat. fat), 32 mg chol., 1552 mg sodium, 45 g carb., 7 g dietary fiber, 24 g protein.

Meatball and Vegetable Soup with Pasta: Prepare as above, except substitute one 12- to 16-ounce package frozen cooked meatballs for the beef tips.

barley-beef SOUP

Prep: 25 minutes
Cook: 1¾ hours
Makes: 8 servings

12 ounces beef or lamb stew
   meat, cut into 1-inch
   cubes
1 tablespoon cooking oil
4 14-ounce cans beef broth
1 cup chopped onion
   (1 large)
½ cup chopped celery
   (1 stalk)
1 teaspoon dried oregano
   or basil, crushed
¼ teaspoon ground black
   pepper
2 cloves garlic, minced
1 bay leaf
1 cup frozen mixed
   vegetables
1 14.5-ounce can diced
   tomatoes, undrained
1 cup ½-inch slices peeled
   parsnip or ½-inch cubes
   peeled potato
⅔ cup quick-cooking barley

1 In a Dutch oven, brown meat in hot oil. Stir in broth, onion, celery, oregano, pepper, garlic, and bay leaf. Bring to boiling; reduce heat. Simmer, covered, for 1½ hours for beef (45 minutes for lamb).

2 Stir in frozen vegetables, tomatoes, parsnip, and barley. Return to boiling; reduce heat. Simmer, covered, for about 15 minutes more or until meat and vegetables are tender. Discard bay leaf.

Nutrition facts per serving: 171 cal., 4 g total fat (1 g sat. fat), 25 mg chol., 865 mg sodium, 20 g carb., 4 g dietary fiber, 13 g protein.

Slow Cooker Directions: Substitute regular barley for quick-cooking barley. In a large skillet, brown cubed beef in hot oil. Drain off fat. In a 5- to 6-quart slow cooker, combine beef and remaining ingredients. Cover and cook on low-heat setting for 8 to 10 hours or on high-heat setting for 4 to 5 hours.

beef GOULASH SOUP

Prep: 30 minutes
Cook: 20 minutes
Makes: 4 servings

- 6 **ounces boneless beef top sirloin steak**
- 1 **teaspoon olive oil**
- ½ **cup chopped onion (1 medium)**
- 2 **cups water**
- 1 **14.5-ounce can no-salt-added diced tomatoes, undrained**
- 1 **14-ounce can beef broth**
- ½ **cup thinly sliced carrot (1 medium)**
- 1 **teaspoon unsweetened cocoa powder**
- 1 **clove garlic, minced**
- 1 **cup thinly sliced cabbage**
- 1 **ounce dried wide noodles (about ½ cup)**
- 2 **teaspoons paprika**
- ¼ **cup light sour cream**
  Snipped fresh parsley (optional)
  Paprika (optional)

1 Trim fat from meat. Cut meat into ½-inch pieces. In a large saucepan, cook and stir meat in hot oil over medium-high heat for about 6 minutes or until meat is brown. Add onion; cook and stir about 3 minutes more or until tender.

2 Stir in the water, tomatoes, broth, carrot, cocoa powder, and garlic. Bring to boiling; reduce heat. Simmer, uncovered, for about 15 minutes or until meat is tender.

3 Stir in cabbage, noodles, and the 2 teaspoons paprika. Simmer, uncovered, for 5 to 7 minutes more or until noodles are tender but still firm.

4 Serve with sour cream. If desired, sprinkle with parsley and additional paprika.

Nutrition facts per serving: 188 cal., 7 g total fat (3 g sat. fat), 36 mg chol., 397 mg sodium, 16 g carb., 3 g dietary fiber, 14 g protein.

teriyaki BEEF SOUP

Start to Finish: 30 minutes
Makes: 5 servings

8 ounces sirloin steak

1 large shallot, cut into
    thin rings

2 teaspoons olive oil

2 14-ounce cans reduced-
    sodium beef broth

1 cup water

½ cup apple juice or
    apple cider

2 medium carrots, cut into
    thin bite-size strips
    (1 cup)

⅓ cup instant brown rice or
    quick-cooking barley

2 tablespoons light
    teriyaki sauce

1 tablespoon grated
    fresh ginger

3 cloves garlic, minced

¼ teaspoon crushed
    red pepper

2 cups coarsely chopped
    broccoli

1 If desired, partially freeze steak for easier slicing. Trim fat from steak. Cut steak into thin bite-size strips. In a large saucepan, cook and stir steak and shallot in hot oil over medium-high heat for 2 to 3 minutes or until beef is brown. Remove beef mixture with a slotted spoon; set aside.

2 In the same saucepan, combine the broth, water, apple juice, carrots, brown rice or barley, teriyaki sauce, ginger, garlic, and crushed red pepper. Bring to boiling; reduce heat. Simmer, covered, for 10 minutes.

3 Stir in broccoli and the beef mixture. Bring to boiling; reduce heat. Simmer, covered, for 3 to 5 minutes or until rice and vegetables are tender.

Nutrition facts per serving: 162 cal., 4 g total fat (1 g sat. fat), 28 mg chol., 481 mg sodium, 18 g carb., 2 g dietary fiber, 13 g protein.

mustard-herb BEEF STEW

Prep: 30 minutes
Cook: 1 hour
Makes: 8 servings

⅓ cup all-purpose flour

1 tablespoon snipped fresh
  Italian (flat-leaf) parsley

1 teaspoon snipped fresh
  thyme, or ½ teaspoon
  dried thyme, crushed

1 teaspoon ground black
  pepper

¼ teaspoon salt

1½ pound boneless beef
  chuck, cut in 1- to
  1½-inch pieces

2 tablespoons olive oil

1 medium onion, peeled
  and cut in wedges

4 carrots, peeled and cut in
  1-inch pieces

1 8-ounce package fresh
  cremini mushrooms,
  halved

8 small Yukon gold
  potatoes, halved

3 tablespoons tomato paste

2 tablespoons spicy brown
  mustard

1 14-ounce can reduced-
  sodium beef broth

1 12-ounce bottle dark
  porter beer or
  nonalcoholic beer

1 bay leaf

1 In large bowl or plastic bag, combine flour, parsley, thyme, pepper, and salt. Add beef, a few pieces at a time; stir or shake to coat. Reserve leftover flour mixture.

2 In a 6-quart Dutch oven, heat oil over medium-high heat. Brown beef in hot oil. Stir in onions, carrots, mushrooms, and potatoes. Cook and stir for 3 minutes. Stir in tomato paste, mustard, and the remaining flour mixture. Add broth, beer, and bay leaf. Bring to boiling; reduce heat. Cover and simmer for 1 to 1¼ hours or until beef is tender. Discard bay leaf.

Nutrition facts per serving: 338 cal., 8 g total fat (2 g sat. fat), 37 mg chol., 538 mg sodium, 36 g carb., 4 g dietary fiber, 25 g protein.

beef STEW WITH RED WINE GRAVY

Prep: 30 minutes
Cook: 12 to 14 hours
(low) or 6 to
7 hours (high)
Makes: 6 servings

- ¼ cup all-purpose flour
- 2 teaspoons dried Italian seasoning
- 1 teaspoon salt
- ½ teaspoon ground black pepper
- 2 pounds boneless beef chuck roast, cut into 1-inch cubes
- 2 tablespoons olive oil
- 2 large onions, cut into thin wedges
- 8 ounces parsnips, quartered lengthwise and halved
- 8 ounces carrots, quartered lengthwise and halved
- 8 ounces Jerusalem artichokes (sunchokes), peeled and coarsely chopped
- 1 cup red wine or beef broth
- ½ cup beef broth
- ¼ cup tomato paste

  Chopped roma tomatoes, golden raisins, and/or red wine vinegar or balsamic vinegar

1 In a plastic bag, combine flour, Italian seasoning, salt, and pepper. Add meat cubes, a few at a time, shaking to coat. In a large skillet, brown meat, half at a time, in hot oil over medium-high heat. Drain off fat.

2 In a 4½- to 6-quart slow cooker, combine onions, parsnips, carrots, and artichokes; top with meat. Pour wine and broth over meat in cooker.

3 Cover and cook on low-heat setting for 12 to 14 hours or on high-heat setting for 6 to 7 hours. Stir in tomato paste. Top individual servings with tomatoes, raisins, and/or vinegar.

Nutrition facts per serving: 215 cal., 4 g total fat (1 g sat. fat), 64 mg chol., 405 mg sodium, 7 g carb., 1 g dietary fiber, 26 g protein.

beef AND BEAN RAGOUT

Prep: 10 minutes
Cook: 8 to 10 hours (low)
     or 4 to 5 hours
     (high)
Makes: 6 servings

1 **pound beef stew meat, cut into ¾- to 1-inch pieces**

1 **16-ounce can kidney beans, rinsed and drained**

1 **15-ounce can tomato sauce with onion and garlic**

1 **14.5-ounce can Italian-style stewed tomatoes, undrained**

½ **of a 28-ounce package frozen diced hash brown potatoes with onions and peppers (about 4 cups)**

Fresh oregano leaves (optional)

1 In a 3½- or 4-quart slow cooker, combine meat, beans, tomato sauce, tomatoes, and potatoes.

2 Cover and cook on low-heat setting for 8 to 10 hours or on high-heat setting for 4 to 5 hours. If desired, garnish each serving with oregano.

Nutrition facts per serving: 260 cal., 3 g total fat (1 g sat. fat), 45 mg chol., 835 mg sodium, 35 g carb., 7 g dietary fiber, 23 g protein.

spicy HAM AND BEAN SOUP

The sour cream and cilantro are optional but adding them makes this recipe truly spectacular. If desired, pass hot sauce at the table for those who really like their food spicy.

Prep: 40 minutes
Cook: 25 minutes
Makes: 8 servings

- 2 **tablespoons vegetable oil**
- 1 **cup chopped onion (1 large)**
- 1 **cup sliced carrots (2 medium)**
- ½ **cup sliced celery (1 stalk)**
- ½ **cup chopped red and/or green sweet pepper (1 small)**
- 6 **cloves garlic, minced**
- 4 **cups beef broth**
- 2 **cups water**
- 2 **cups cubed cooked ham (10 ounces)**
- 1 **15-ounce can black beans, rinsed and drained**
- 1 **15-ounce can red kidney beans, rinsed and drained**
- 2 **teaspoons ground cumin**
- 1 **teaspoon dried thyme, crushed**
- ⅛ **to ¼ teaspoon cayenne pepper**
- ⅛ **teaspoon ground black pepper**
- ½ **cup dry white wine (optional)**
  Sour cream (optional)
  Fresh cilantro leaves (optional)

1 In a 4- to 6-quart Dutch oven, heat oil over medium-high heat. Add onion, carrots, celery, sweet pepper, and garlic; cook about 5 minutes or until onion is tender.

2 Stir in broth, the water, ham, black beans, kidney beans, cumin, thyme, cayenne, and black pepper. If desired, stir in wine. Bring to boiling; reduce heat. Cover and simmer for 25 to 30 minutes or until carrot is tender. If desired, serve with sour cream and garnish with cilantro.

Nutrition facts per serving: 204 cal., 6 g total fat (1 g sat. fat), 23 mg chol., 1247 mg sodium, 21 g carb., 7 g dietary fiber, 19 g protein.

asian PORK SOUP

Start to Finish: 25 minutes
Makes: 6 servings

1 tablespoon canola oil

12 ounces lean boneless pork, cut into thin bite-size strips

2 cups sliced fresh shiitake mushrooms

2 cloves garlic, minced

3 14-ounce cans reduced-sodium chicken broth

2 tablespoons dry sherry

2 tablespoons reduced-sodium soy sauce

2 teaspoons grated fresh ginger, or ½ teaspoon ground ginger

¼ teaspoon crushed red pepper

2 cups shredded napa cabbage

1 scallion, thinly sliced

Fresh cilantro sprigs (optional)

1 In a large saucepan, heat oil over medium heat. Add pork; cook and stir for 2 to 3 minutes or until slightly pink in center. Remove from pan. Add mushrooms and garlic to saucepan; cook until tender.

2 Stir in chicken broth, sherry, soy sauce, ginger, and crushed red pepper. Bring to boiling. Stir in pork, napa cabbage, and scallion; heat through. If desired, garnish individual servings with cilantro.

Nutrition facts per serving: 160 cal., 6 g total fat (1 g sat. fat), 31 mg chol., 691 mg sodium, 10 g carb., 1 g dietary fiber, 16 g protein.

tex-mex PORK AND CORN SOUP

Start to Finish: 40 minutes
Makes: 5 servings

- 1 tablespoon olive oil
- 12 ounces pork tenderloin or lean boneless pork, cut into bite-size pieces
- 1 cup chopped red onion
- 4 cloves garlic, minced
- 1 10-ounce package frozen whole kernel corn
- 1 14-ounce can reduced-sodium chicken broth
- 1¾ cups water
- 1 cup purchased chipotle-style salsa or regular salsa
- 1 cup chopped red and/or yellow sweet pepper
- ½ cup chopped tomato
- 3 tablespoons sour cream (optional)
- Snipped fresh cilantro (optional)

1 In a large saucepan, heat oil over medium-high heat. Add pork strips; cook and stir for 4 to 5 minutes or until brown and juices run clear. Remove pork strips from saucepan. Add red onion and garlic to saucepan. Cook and stir for 3 to 4 minutes or until onion is tender.

2 Add corn to saucepan. Cook and stir for 4 minutes. Stir in chicken broth, water, salsa, and sweet pepper. Bring to boiling; reduce heat. Simmer, uncovered, for 10 minutes. Return pork strips to saucepan; heat through. Remove saucepan from heat; stir in tomato. If desired, top individual servings with sour cream and cilantro.

Nutrition facts per serving: 192 cal., 5 g total fat (1 g sat. fat), 44 mg chol., 539 mg sodium, 21 g carb., 3 g dietary fiber, 19 g protein.

spicy PORK AND VEGETABLE SOUP

This sophisticated and tasty soup is packed full of winter vegetables. Fresh spinach added prior to serving adds a touch of color and a boost of nutrition.

Prep: 30 minutes
Cook: 10 to 11 hours
   (low) or 5 to
   5½ hours (high)
Makes: 6 servings

1 **pound lean pork or beef stew meat**

1 **tablespoon canola oil**

½ **cup chopped onion (1 medium)**

1 **teaspoon paprika**

2 **cloves garlic, minced**

3 **cups reduced-sodium beef broth**

8 **ounces winter squash, peeled and cut into ½-inch pieces**

3 **medium parsnips or carrots, cut into ¼-inch slices (1½ cups)**

1 **medium sweet potato, peeled and cut into ½-inch pieces**

1 **8.75-ounce can whole kernel corn, undrained**

¼ **teaspoon salt**

¼ **teaspoon cayenne pepper**

2 **cups torn fresh spinach**

1 Cut meat into ½-inch pieces. In a large skillet, cook half of the meat in hot oil over medium heat until brown. Transfer meat to a 3½- or 4-quart slow cooker. Add the remaining meat, the onion, paprika, and garlic to skillet. Cook until meat is brown and onion is tender. Drain off fat. Transfer meat mixture to cooker.

2 Stir broth, squash, parsnips, sweet potato, corn, salt, and cayenne into meat mixture in cooker. Cover and cook on low-heat setting for 10 to 11 hours or on high-heat setting for 5 to 5½ hours. Just before serving, stir in spinach.

Nutrition facts per serving: 227 cal., 8 g total fat (2 g sat. fat), 41 mg chol., 488 mg sodium, 19 g carb., 4 g dietary fiber, 20 g protein.

corn-sausage CHOWDER

A tossed green salad and slices of your favorite bakery bread are all you need to finish off this meal.

Start to Finish: 50 minutes
Makes: 6 servings

1 **pound bulk pork sausage**

1 **medium onion, chopped**

3 **medium potatoes, cut into ½-inch cubes**

2 **cups water**

1 **teaspoon dried basil or Italian seasoning, crushed**

½ **teaspoon ground black pepper**

1 **15.25-ounce can whole kernel corn, drained**

1 **14.75-ounce can cream-style corn**

1 **12-ounce can evaporated milk (1½ cups)**

1 In a 4-quart Dutch oven, cook pork sausage over medium heat for 5 minutes. Add onion; cook for about 5 minutes more or until sausage is brown. Drain off fat.

2 Add potatoes, the water, basil, and pepper. Bring to boiling; reduce heat. Cover and simmer for about 20 minutes or until potato is tender.

3 Stir in whole kernel corn, cream-style corn, and evaporated milk; heat through.

Nutrition facts per serving: 436 cal., 22 g total fat (3 g sat. fat), 19 mg chol., 408 mg sodium, 38 g carb., 4 g dietary fiber, 20 g protein.

cider PORK STEW

Apple cider or juice and an apple give this fix-and-forget stew a captivating hint of sweetness.

Prep: 20 minutes
Cook: 10 to 12 hours
(low) or 5 to 6
hours (high)
Makes: 8 servings

2 pounds pork shoulder
roast, cut into 1-inch
cubes

3 medium potatoes, cubed

3 medium carrots, cut into
½-inch pieces

2 medium onions, sliced

1 medium apple, cored and
coarsely chopped

½ cup coarsely chopped
celery

3 tablespoons quick-cooking
tapioca

2 cups apple cider or
apple juice

1 teaspoon salt

1 teaspoon caraway seeds

¼ teaspoon ground black
pepper

Celery leaves (optional)

1 In a 3½- to 5½-quart slow cooker, combine pork, potatoes, carrots, onions, apple, celery, and tapioca. Stir in apple cider, salt, caraway seeds, and pepper.

2 Cover and cook on low-heat setting for 10 to 12 hours or on high-heat setting for 5 to 6 hours. If desired, garnish individual servings with celery leaves.

Nutrition facts per serving: 272 cal., 7 g total fat (2 g sat. fat), 73 mg chol., 405 mg sodium, 27 g carb., 3 g dietary fiber, 24 g protein.

brunswick-style STEW

Prep: 20 minutes
Cook: 8 to 10 hours (low)
        or 4 to 5 hours
        (high)
Makes: 6 to 8 servings

1½ **to 2 pounds meaty
     smoked pork hocks**

1 **14.5-ounce can diced
    tomatoes, undrained**

1 **14-ounce can chicken
    broth**

3 **medium onions, cut into
    thin wedges**

½ **cup ketchup**

¼ **cup cider vinegar**

2 **tablespoons packed
    brown sugar**

2 **tablespoons
    Worcestershire sauce**

4 **cloves garlic, minced**

¼ **teaspoon ground black
    pepper**

¼ **teaspoon hot pepper
    sauce**

1½ **cups frozen baby lima
     beans**

1 **cup frozen whole kernel
    corn**

1 In a 5- to 6-quart slow cooker, combine pork hocks, tomatoes, broth, onions, ketchup, vinegar, brown sugar, Worcestershire sauce, garlic, black pepper, and hot pepper sauce.

2 Cover and cook on low-heat setting for 8 to 10 hours or on high-heat setting for 4 to 5 hours.

3 Remove pork hocks. When cool enough to handle, cut meat off bones; coarsely chop meat. Discard bones. Return meat to cooker.

4 If using low-heat setting, turn to high-heat setting. Stir in frozen lima beans and frozen corn. Cover and cook for 30 minutes more.

Nutrition facts per serving: 224 cal., 4 g total fat (1 g sat. fat), 20 mg chol., 1138 mg sodium, 37 g carb., 4 g dietary fiber, 11 g protein.

italian PORK STEW

Two kinds of pork make this hearty stew extra-flavorful. Mop up the wine-flavored gravy with chunks of Italian bread or rolls.

Prep: 35 minutes
Stand: 1 hour
Cook: 7 to 8 hours (low)
      or 3½ to 4 hours
      (high)
Makes: 6 servings

- 2 **cups dried Great Northern beans**
- 6 **cups cold water**
- 8 **ounces Italian sausage (remove casings, if present)**
- 1 **pound lean boneless pork, trimmed and cut into ½-inch pieces**
- 1½ **cups coarsely chopped onions**
- 3 **medium-size carrots, cut into ½-inch pieces**
- 3 **cloves garlic, chopped**
- 3 **cups water**
- 1 **teaspoon instant beef bouillon granules**
- ½ **teaspoon dried thyme**
- ½ **teaspoon dried oregano**
- ¼ **cup dry red wine or water**
- ⅓ **cup (½ of a 6-ounce can) tomato paste**
- ¼ **cup chopped fresh parsley**

1. Rinse beans; drain. In a large saucepan, combine beans and the 6 cups water. Bring to a boil; reduce heat. Simmer, uncovered, for 10 minutes. Remove from heat. Cover and let stand for 1 hour. Drain and rinse beans. Transfer beans to 4- to 5-quart slow cooker.

2. In a large skillet, cook sausage over medium heat until cooked through, stirring to break sausage into bite-size pieces. Using a slotted spoon, transfer sausage to slow cooker, reserving drippings in skillet. In the same skillet, cook pork, half at a time, until browned. Drain off fat. Transfer to slow cooker. Add onions, carrots, and garlic to slow cooker. Stir in the 3 cups water, bouillon granules, thyme, and oregano.

3. Cover and cook on low-heat setting for 7 to 8 hours or on high-heat setting for 3½ to 4 hours.

4. If necessary, raise temperature to high-heat setting. In small bowl, stir wine into tomato paste; add to mixture in slow cooker along with parsley. Cover slow cooker; cook for 15 minutes longer.

Nutrition facts per serving: 473 cal., 13 g total fat (5 g sat. fat), 73 mg chol., 566 mg sodium, 49 g carb., 15 g dietary fiber, 37 g protein.

pork STEW WITH POLENTA

Italian seasoning dresses tender chunks of pork with spinach, peppers, and onions in a tomato broth. Spooned over hot polenta and given a dusting of shredded Parmesan, this stew is a fine main-dish meal.

Prep: 20 minutes
Cook: 7 to 8 hours (low)
or 3½ to 4 hours
(high)
Makes: 4 servings

1½ **pounds boneless pork country-style ribs**

1 **cup chopped onion (1 large)**

1 **cup coarsely chopped green, yellow, and/or red sweet pepper (1 large)**

1 **14.5-ounce can diced tomatoes with basil and oregano, undrained**

1 **14-ounce can beef broth**

¼ **cup dry red wine**

3 **tablespoons quick-cooking tapioca, crushed**

1 **teaspoon dried Italian seasoning, crushed**

¼ **teaspoon salt**

2 **cloves garlic, minced**

1 **16-ounce tube refrigerated polenta**

2 **cups torn baby spinach (optional)**

Shredded Parmesan cheese (optional)

1 Trim fat from meat. Cut meat into 1½- to 2-inch pieces. In a 3½- or 4-quart slow cooker, combine meat, onion, and sweet pepper. Stir in tomatoes, broth, red wine, tapioca, Italian seasoning, salt, and garlic.

2 Cover and cook on low-heat setting for 7 to 8 hours or on high-heat setting for 3½ to 4 hours.

3 Meanwhile, prepare polenta according to package directions.

4 Just before serving, if desired, stir spinach into stew. Serve stew with polenta. If desired, sprinkle each serving with Parmesan cheese.

Nutrition facts per serving: 450 cal., 17 g total fat (5 g sat. fat), 116 mg chol., 1342 mg sodium, 32 g carb., 2 g dietary fiber, 39 g protein.

pork STEW WITH GREMOLATA

Prep: 30 minutes
Cook: 1 hour
Makes: 4 servings

- 3 tablespoons all-purpose flour
- ½ teaspoon ground black pepper
- ¼ teaspoon salt
- 1 pound boneless pork or veal sirloin, trimmed and cut into 1-inch cubes
- 2 tablespoons olive oil
- ½ cup dry white wine
- 1 large onion, cut into wedges
- 1 teaspoon bottled minced garlic (2 cloves)
- 1 14.5-ounce can diced tomatoes, undrained
- 1 14-ounce can beef broth
- 2 carrots, peeled and bias-sliced
- 2 stalks celery, chopped
- ¼ teaspoon dried thyme, crushed
- 1 bay leaf
- 1 strip (4x1-inch) lemon peel
  Gremolata*
- 1 cup dried orzo, cooked according to package directions and drained
  Lemon zest (optional)

1 Place flour, pepper, and salt in a plastic bag. Add meat cubes, a few at a time, shaking to coat. In a large saucepan or Dutch oven, heat 1 tablespoon of the olive oil. Add meat; cook until meat is browned. Transfer meat from saucepan to a medium bowl. Remove saucepan from heat; add wine. Return to heat; cook for 1 minute, stirring to scrape up browned bits. Add wine mixture to meat in bowl.

2 Add remaining oil to saucepan. Add onion; cook over medium heat for 3 to 4 minutes or until tender. Stir in garlic; cook and stir for 1 minute. Stir in meat mixture, tomatoes, beef broth, carrots, celery, thyme, bay leaf, and lemon peel. Bring to boiling; reduce heat. Cover and simmer for about 1 hour or until meat is tender.

3 If desired, uncover stew and cook for 5 to 10 minutes more or until stew thickens slightly. Discard bay leaf and lemon peel strip. Serve stew with Gremolata and hot cooked orzo. If desired, garnish with lemon zest.

*Gremolata: In a small bowl, stir together ¼ cup snipped fresh flat-leaf parsley, 2 teaspoons finely shredded lemon zest, and 2 teaspoons bottled minced garlic (4 cloves).

Nutrition facts per serving: 491 cal., 14 g total fat (3 g sat. fat), 71 mg chol., 748 mg sodium, 51 g carb., 4 g dietary fiber, 33 g protein.

southwest PORK STEW

Start to Finish: 25 minutes
Makes: 4 servings

12 ounces boneless pork loin or sirloin, cut into bite-size strips

1 14-ounce can reduced-sodium chicken broth

1 6-ounce can no-salt-added tomato paste

½ cup bottled cilantro-flavored salsa*

½ teaspoon ground cumin

1 medium zucchini, halved lengthwise and thinly sliced (2 cups)

1 cup frozen sweet soybeans (edamame) or baby lima beans

½ cup peeled, pitted, and chopped mango (1 small)

Lightly coat a large saucepan with cooking spray. Cook and stir pork in hot pan over medium-high heat for about 2 minutes or until brown. Stir in broth, tomato paste, salsa, and cumin. Stir in zucchini and edamame. Bring to boiling; reduce heat. Cover and simmer for about 10 minutes or until vegetables are tender. Top with chopped mango.

Nutrition facts per serving: 243 cal., 7 g total fat (2 g sat. fat), 47 mg chol., 594 mg sodium, 19 g carb., 6 g dietary fiber, 26 g protein.

*Tip: If you can't find cilantro-flavored salsa, use regular salsa and stir in 2 tablespoons snipped fresh cilantro.

lamb CURRY

Prep: 20 minutes
Cook: 1½ hours
Makes: 8 servings

3 pounds lamb shoulder

3 tablespoons olive oil or cooking oil

½ cup chopped onion (1 medium)

2 tablespoons all-purpose flour

2 tablespoons curry powder

2 cups chicken broth

2¼ cups coarsely chopped tomato (3 medium)

2 cups peeled and diced celery root

1 cup whipping cream

1⅓ cups coarsely chopped and peeled Golden Delicious or other cooking apple (2 medium)

¾ cup coarsely chopped tomato (1 medium)

Hot cooked rice (optional)

Desired condiments (such as chutney, toasted shredded coconut, or chopped apple or nuts)

1 Trim fat from lamb. Cut lamb into 1-inch cubes, discarding bone.

2 In a large saucepan or Dutch oven, brown lamb, one-third at a time, in hot oil, cooking onion with last portion of lamb. Stir in flour; cook for 7 minutes, stirring frequently. Stir in curry powder; stir in broth. Add the 2¼ cups chopped tomato and the celery root. Bring to boiling; reduce heat. Simmer, covered, about 1½ hours or until meat is tender.

3 Stir in whipping cream. Simmer, uncovered, for 2 minutes more. Stir in apple and the remaining ¾ cup chopped tomato. Heat through. If desired, serve with rice and desired condiments.

Nutrition facts per serving: 434 cal., 25 g total fat (10 g sat. fat), 99 mg chol., 298 mg sodium, 32 g carb., 3 g dietary fiber, 22 g protein.

lamb CASSOULET

Prep: 30 minutes
Stand: 1 hour
Cook: 1½ hours
Makes: 6 servings

2 **cups dried navy beans**

8 **cups water**

1 **pound lean boneless lamb, cut into 1-inch cubes**

1 **tablespoon vegetable oil**

1 **cup chopped carrots (2 medium)**

½ **cup chopped green sweet pepper (1 medium)**

½ **cup chopped onion (1 medium)**

1 **tablespoon instant beef bouillon granules**

1 **tablespoon Worcestershire sauce**

2 **teaspoons snipped fresh thyme, or 1 teaspoon dried thyme, crushed**

3 **cloves garlic, minced**

2 **bay leaves**

4 **cups water**

8 **ounces skinless, boneless chicken thighs, cut into 1-inch pieces**

1 **14.5-ounce can diced tomatoes, undrained**

½ **teaspoon salt**

Ground black pepper

1 Rinse and drain beans. In a large pot, combine beans and the 8 cups water. Bring to boiling; reduce heat. Simmer, uncovered, for 2 minutes. Remove from heat. Cover and let stand for 1 hour. (Or, place beans in water in pot. Cover and let soak in a cool place for 6 to 8 hours or overnight.) Drain and rinse beans. Wipe pot dry.

2 In the same pot, brown lamb, half at a time, in hot oil; drain fat. Return all lamb to the pot. Add beans, carrots, sweet pepper, onion, bouillon granules, Worcestershire sauce, dried thyme (if using), garlic, and bay leaves to the pot. Add the 4 cups water. Bring to boiling; reduce heat. Simmer, covered, for 1 to 1½ hours or until beans are tender.

3 Stir in chicken, tomatoes, salt, and (if using) fresh thyme. Return to boiling; reduce heat. Simmer, uncovered, for 30 minutes more. Discard bay leaves. Skim fat if necessary. Season to taste with salt and black pepper.

Nutrition facts per serving: 417 cal., 8 g total fat (2 g sat. fat), 79 mg chol., 899 mg sodium, 49 g carb., 18 g dietary fiber, 39 g protein.

lamb STEW WITH PASTA

Prep: 25 minutes
Cook: 1 hour
Makes: 4 servings

1 pound lamb or beef
  stew meat

1 medium onion, sliced and
  separated into rings

2 tablespoons cooking oil

3½ cups water

¼ cup snipped sun-dried
  tomatoes (not oil-packed)

1 teaspoon dried Italian
  seasoning, crushed

¼ teaspoon salt

¼ teaspoon ground black
  pepper

2 cups sliced fresh
  mushrooms

1 9-ounce package frozen
  cut green beans

1 cup thinly sliced carrots
  (2 medium)

¾ cup dried medium bow-
  tie pasta

1 15-ounce can tomato
  sauce

1 In a large saucepan, cook the lamb and onion in hot oil until the meat is brown.

2 Stir water, dried tomatoes, Italian seasoning, salt, and pepper into the saucepan. Bring to boiling; reduce heat. Simmer, covered, for about 45 minutes (or about 1¼ hours for beef, if using) or until the meat is nearly tender.

3 Stir mushrooms, green beans, carrots, and pasta into meat mixture. Return to boiling; reduce heat. Simmer, covered, for 15 minutes more or until meat, vegetables, and pasta are tender. Stir in tomato sauce; heat through.

Nutrition facts per serving: 309 cal., 12 g total fat (2 g sat. fat), 71 mg chol., 803 mg sodium, 24 g carb., 5 g dietary fiber, 29 g protein.

fish
AND SEAFOOD

Manhattan Clam Chowder, *page 113*

chunky FISH SOUP

Prep: 25 minutes
Cook: 20 minutes
Makes: 6 servings

½ **cup chopped onion
(1 medium)**

½ **cup chopped celery
(1 stalk)**

½ **cup chopped carrot
(1 medium)**

1 **clove garlic, minced**

2 **tablespoons olive oil**

5 **cups vegetable broth**

1 **14.5-ounce can diced
tomatoes, undrained**

1½ **pounds assorted white
fish, cut into bite-size
pieces (such as halibut,
red snapper, or cod)**

2 **tablespoons snipped
fresh Italian (flat-leaf)
parsley**

6 **slices country-style bread,
toasted**

1 In a Dutch oven, cook onion, celery, carrot, and garlic in hot oil over medium-high heat for about 5 minutes or until tender. Add broth and tomatoes. Heat to boiling; reduce heat. Simmer, covered, for 15 minutes. Stir in fish. Simmer, covered, for about 5 minutes more or until fish begins to flake when tested with a fork. Stir in parsley.

2 Serve with toasted bread.

Nutrition facts per serving: 286 cal., 8 g total fat (1 g sat. fat), 36 mg chol., 1146 mg sodium, 23 g carb., 2 g dietary fiber, 27 g protein.

seafood MINESTRONE

Start to Finish: 30 minutes
Makes: 4 to 6 servings

- 2 cloves garlic, minced
- 1 tablespoon extra-virgin olive oil
- 2 leeks, halved lengthwise and sliced ½ inch thick
- 2 14-ounce cans reduced-sodium chicken broth
- 2 cups water
- 1 15-ounce can navy beans, rinsed and drained
- 1 teaspoon dried thyme, crushed
- 4 ounces broken dried fettuccine or linguine
- 1 pound peeled and deveined medium shrimp and/or bay scallops
- 4 medium roma tomatoes, coarsely chopped
- 1 cup arugula or spinach
  Ground black pepper

1. In a 4-quart Dutch oven, cook garlic in hot oil for 15 seconds; add leeks. Cook and stir until tender. Add broth, water, beans, and thyme. Bring to boiling. Add pasta; simmer, uncovered, for 10 to 12 minutes or until pasta is just tender, stirring occasionally.

2. Stir in seafood; simmer for 2 minutes or until seafood is opaque. Divide among soup plates. Add tomatoes and arugula. Season to taste with pepper.

Nutrition facts per serving: 442 cal., 7 g total fat (1 g sat. fat), 172 mg chol., 1138 mg sodium, 57 g carb., 9 g dietary fiber, 42 g protein.

quick CIOPPINO WITH BASIL GREMOLATA

Start to Finish: 25 minutes
Makes: 4 servings

- 6 ounces fresh or frozen cod fillets
- 6 ounces fresh or frozen peeled and deveined shrimp
- 1 cup green sweet pepper strips (1 medium)
- 1 cup chopped onion (1 large)
- 2 cloves garlic, minced
- 1 tablespoon olive oil or vegetable oil
- 2 14.5-ounce cans Italian-style stewed tomatoes, undrained and cut up
- ½ cup water
- ¼ teaspoon salt
- ¼ teaspoon ground black pepper
- 3 tablespoons snipped fresh basil
- 1 tablespoon finely shredded lemon zest
- 2 cloves garlic, minced

1 Thaw cod and shrimp, if frozen. Rinse cod and shrimp; pat dry with paper towels. Cut cod into 1-inch pieces. In a large pot, cook and stir sweet pepper, onion, and 2 cloves minced garlic in hot oil until tender. Stir in tomatoes, water, salt, and black pepper. Bring to boiling. Stir in cod and shrimp. Return to boiling; reduce heat. Simmer, covered, for 2 to 3 minutes or until cod flakes easily when tested with a fork and shrimp turn opaque.

2 In a small bowl, combine basil, lemon zest, and remaining minced garlic. Sprinkle each serving with basil mixture.

Nutrition facts per serving: 188 cal., 5 g total fat (1 g sat. fat), 83 mg chol., 921 mg sodium, 20 g carb., 5 g dietary fiber, 19 g protein.

red PEPPER AND SNAPPER SOUP

When you need a no-fail main dish, rely on this rich-tasting, easy-to-assemble fish soup.
If red snapper or orange roughy isn't available, try it with cod or sole.

Start to Finish: 50 minutes
Makes: 5 servings

1¼ **pounds fresh or frozen skinless red snapper, orange roughy, or other firm-fleshed fish fillets**

2 **tablespoons olive oil**

3 **medium red sweet peppers, coarsely chopped (2¼ cups)**

1 **cup chopped shallots or onions**

3 **14.5-ounce cans reduced-sodium chicken broth (5¼ cups total)**

¼ **teaspoon salt**

¼ **teaspoon ground black pepper**

⅛ **teaspoon ground red pepper**

½ **cup snipped fresh Italian parsley**

Fresh Italian parsley sprigs (optional)

1 Thaw fish, if frozen. Rinse fish; pat dry. Cut fish into 1-inch pieces. In a large saucepan or Dutch oven, heat oil over medium heat. Add sweet peppers and shallots; cook for 5 minutes. Carefully add 1 can of the broth. Bring to boiling; reduce heat. Cover and simmer for about 20 minutes or until peppers are very tender. Remove from heat; cool slightly.

2 Pour half of the sweet pepper mixture into a blender container. Cover and blend until nearly smooth. Pour into a medium bowl. Repeat with remaining pepper mixture. Return all to saucepan. Add remaining chicken broth, the salt, black pepper, and ground red pepper. Bring to boiling; reduce heat. Add fish to broth mixture. Cover and simmer for about 5 minutes or until fish flakes easily when tested with a fork, stirring once or twice. Stir in snipped parsley. If desired, garnish soup with parsley sprigs.

Nutrition facts per serving: 223 cal., 8 g total fat (1 g sat. fat), 42 mg chol., 859 mg sodium, 10 g carb., 0 g dietary fiber, 27 g protein.

creamy SEAFOOD SOUP WITH BASIL

Prep: 30 minutes
Cook: 25 minutes
Makes: 8 appetizer
　　servings

2 pounds live mussels in
　shells, or 12 ounces fresh
　small shrimp in shells

12 quarts (48 cups) cold
　water

1 cup salt

1 14-ounce can reduced-
　sodium chicken broth

1½ cups water

1 tablespoon olive oil

1 cup finely chopped leeks
　(3 medium)

2 cloves garlic, minced

¼ teaspoon saffron threads,
　or ⅛ teaspoon ground
　turmeric

¼ teaspoon ground black
　pepper

1 cup fat-free half-and-half

1 tablespoon finely
　shredded fresh basil

1 If using mussels, scrub live mussels under cold running water. Using your fingers, pull out the beards that are visible between the shells. In an extra-large bowl, combine 4 quarts (16 cups) of the cold water and ⅓ cup of the salt. Add mussels; soak for 15 minutes. Drain in a colander. Rinse mussels, discarding water. Repeat two more times with the remaining 8 quarts water and the ⅔ cup salt. Rinse well. (If using shrimp, rinse shrimp. Pat dry with paper towels.)

2 In a Dutch oven, combine broth and the 1½ cups water; bring to boiling. Add mussels; reduce heat. Simmer, covered, for 5 to 7 minutes or until shells open and mussels are cooked through. Discard any mussels that do not open. (If using shrimp, simmer for 2 to 3 minutes or until shells are pink and shrimp are opaque.)

3 Using a slotted spoon, remove mussels or shrimp; set aside until cool enough to handle. Strain cooking liquid through a cheesecloth-lined sieve into a large bowl. Remove meat from mussel shells and set aside, discarding shells. (Or peel and devein shrimp, discarding shells.)

4 In a large saucepan, heat oil over medium heat. Add leeks and garlic; cook and stir for 3 to 5 minutes or until tender. Stir in the reserved cooking liquid, saffron, and pepper. Bring to boiling; reduce heat. Boil gently, uncovered, for about 15 minutes or until reduced to 3 cups. Stir in half-and-half; heat through.

5 Before serving, stir mussels or shrimp into soup. Sprinkle with basil.

Nutrition facts per serving: 79 cal., 4 g total fat (1 g sat. fat), 16 mg chol., 456 mg sodium, 7 g carb., 0 g dietary fiber, 3 g protein.

lemon AND SCALLOP SOUP

Long-stemmed, tiny-capped, and slightly crunchy, enoki mushrooms play an important role in Asian cooking. These elegant mushrooms have a light, fruity flavor. Wait until the last moment to toss them in because they toughen if heated.

Start to Finish: 25 minutes
Makes: 4 servings

- 12 ounces fresh or frozen bay scallops
- 5 cups reduced-sodium chicken broth or fish stock
- ½ cup dry white wine, reduced-sodium chicken broth, or fish stock
- 3 tablespoons snipped fresh cilantro
- 2 teaspoons finely shredded lemon zest
- ¼ teaspoon ground black pepper
- 1 pound asparagus spears, trimmed and cut into bite-size pieces
- 1 cup fresh enoki mushrooms or shiitake mushrooms
- ½ cup sliced scallions
- 1 tablespoon lemon juice

1. Thaw scallops, if frozen. Rinse well and drain; set aside.

2. In a large saucepan, combine broth, wine, cilantro, lemon zest, and pepper. Bring to boiling.

3. Add scallops, asparagus, shiitake mushrooms (if using), and scallions. Return to boiling; reduce heat. Simmer, uncovered, for 3 to 5 minutes or until asparagus is tender and scallops are opaque.

4. Remove saucepan from heat. Stir in the enoki mushrooms (if using) and lemon juice. Serve immediately.

Nutrition facts per serving: 153 cal., 2 g total fat (0 g sat. fat), 28 mg chol., 940 mg sodium, 10 g carb., 2 g dietary fiber, 20 g protein.

crab AND TOMATO BISQUE

Let this elegant, easy bisque star at your next special occasion dinner. Don't tell anyone that it starts with two cans of soup.

Start to Finish: 15 minutes
Makes: 4 servings

1 **19-ounce can ready-to-eat tomato-basil soup**

1 **10.75-ounce can condensed cream of shrimp soup**

1 **cup vegetable broth**

1 **cup half-and-half, light cream, or milk**

1 **tablespoon dried minced onion**

1 **tablespoon snipped fresh parsley, or 1 teaspoon dried parsley flakes**

1 **6.5-ounce can crabmeat, drained, flaked, and cartilage removed**

1 In a large saucepan, combine soups, broth, half-and-half, onion, and dried parsley (if using).

2 Cook over medium heat until bubbly, stirring occasionally. Stir in crabmeat and fresh parsley (if using); heat through.

Nutrition facts per serving: 242 cal., 12 g total fat (6 g sat. fat), 73 mg chol., 1447 mg sodium, 20 g carb., 1 g dietary fiber, 15 g protein.

asian SHRIMP AND VEGETABLE SOUP

Start to Finish: 45 minutes
Makes: 6 servings

12 ounces fresh or frozen large shrimp in shells

4 scallions

2 teaspoons canola oil

2 medium carrots, peeled and thinly sliced

8 ounces fresh shiitake or oyster mushrooms, stemmed and coarsely chopped

1 tablespoon grated fresh ginger, or 1 teaspoon ground ginger

2 cloves garlic, minced

2 14-ounce cans reduced-sodium chicken broth

2 cups water

1 cup frozen sweet soybeans (edamame)

1 tablespoon reduced-sodium soy sauce

¼ teaspoon crushed red pepper (optional)

1 cup trimmed sugar snap peas and/or coarsely shredded bok choy

Slivered scallions (optional)

1 Thaw shrimp, if frozen. Peel and devein shrimp. Rinse shrimp; pat dry with paper towels. Set aside. Diagonally slice the whole scallions into 1-inch-long pieces, keeping white parts separate from green tops. Set green tops aside. In a large nonstick saucepan, heat oil over medium heat. Add white parts of the scallions, the carrots, and mushrooms; cook for 5 minutes, stirring occasionally. Add ginger and garlic; cook and stir for 1 minute more.

2 Add chicken broth, the water, soybeans, soy sauce, and (if desired) crushed red pepper to mushroom mixture. Bring to boiling; reduce heat. Cover and simmer for about 5 minutes or just until carrot is tender.

3 Add shrimp and pea pods and/or bok choy. Return to boiling; reduce heat. Simmer, uncovered, for 2 to 3 minutes or until shrimp are opaque. Stir in scallion tops just before serving. If desired, garnish with slivered scallions.

Nutrition facts per serving: 136 cal., 4 g total fat (0 g sat. fat), 65 mg chol., 489 mg sodium, 10 g carb., 3 g dietary fiber, 16 g protein.

hot-and-sour SOUP

Prep: 20 minutes
Cook: 9 to 11 hours (low)
    or 3 to 4 hours
    (high)
Makes: 8 servings

4   cups chicken broth
1   8-ounce can bamboo
    shoots, drained
1   8-ounce can sliced water
    chestnuts, drained
1   4-ounce can (drained
    weight) sliced
    mushrooms, drained
3   tablespoons quick-
    cooking tapioca
3   tablespoons rice wine
    vinegar or vinegar
1   tablespoon soy sauce
1   teaspoon sugar
½   teaspoon ground black
    pepper
1   8-ounce package frozen
    peeled and deveined
    medium shrimp
4   ounces firm tofu, drained
    and cubed
1   egg, lightly beaten
2   tablespoons snipped
    fresh parsley or cilantro

1 In a 3½- or 4-quart slow cooker, combine broth, bamboo shoots, water chestnuts, mushrooms, tapioca, vinegar, soy sauce, sugar, and pepper.

2 Cover and cook on low-heat setting for 9 to 11 hours or on high-heat setting for 3 to 4 hours. Add frozen shrimp and tofu. Cover and cook on low- or high-heat setting for about 50 minutes more or until shrimp are opaque.

3 Pour beaten egg slowly into soup in a thin stream. Stir soup gently so that egg forms fine strands instead of clumps. Sprinkle each serving with parsley.

Nutrition facts per serving: 114 cal., 2 g total fat (1 g sat. fat), 83 mg chol., 664 mg sodium, 9 g carb., 1 g dietary fiber, 13 g protein.

thai SHRIMP SOUP

Prep: 30 minutes
Cook: 22 minutes
Makes: 4 servings

12 ounces fresh or frozen peeled and deveined shrimp

2 14-ounce cans reduced-sodium chicken broth

1 cup water

2 stalks lemongrass (white part only), cut into ½-inch slices

2 medium fresh jalapeño chile peppers, halved lengthwise and seeded*

1 cup stemmed and sliced fresh shiitake and/or button mushrooms, or ½ of a 15-ounce can whole straw mushrooms, drained

1 cup chopped red sweet pepper

1 cup sliced carrots

2 tablespoons lime juice

2 tablespoons rice vinegar or white wine vinegar

1 tablespoon packed brown sugar

1 tablespoon fish sauce

¼ cup slivered fresh basil

1 Thaw shrimp, if frozen. Rinse shrimp. In a large saucepan, bring broth and water to boiling. Add lemongrass and jalapeños. Return to boiling; reduce heat. Simmer, covered, for 10 minutes. Use a slotted spoon to remove lemongrass and chile peppers; discard.

2 Stir mushrooms, sweet pepper, carrots, lime juice, vinegar, brown sugar, and fish sauce into saucepan. Bring to boiling; reduce heat. Simmer, covered, for 10 to 15 minutes or until vegetables are crisp-tender. Add shrimp. Cook, covered, for 2 to 4 minutes more or until shrimp are opaque. Sprinkle each serving with basil.

Nutrition facts per serving: 170 cal., 2 g total fat (0 g sat. fat), 129 mg chol., 971 mg sodium, 17 g carb., 3 g dietary fiber, 21 g protein.

*Tip: Because chile peppers contain volatile oils that can burn your skin and eyes, avoid direct contact with them as much as possible. When working with chile peppers, wear plastic or rubber gloves. If your bare hands do touch the peppers, wash your hands and nails well with soap and warm water.

red AND GREEN GAZPACHO

This make-ahead chilled soup is a colorful blend of tomatoes, tomatillos, cucumber, shrimp, and cilantro—it's as refreshing as it is easy.

Prep: 30 minutes
Chill: 1 hour
Makes: 6 servings

- **3 cups chopped red and/or partially green tomatoes**
- **½ cup chopped tomatillos**
- **1 16-ounce can tomato juice (2 cups)**
- **½ cup chopped cucumber**
- **1 tablespoon seeded and finely chopped freah jalapeño/chile pepper***
- **¼ cup finely chopped scallion**
- **1 clove garlic, minced**
- **¼ teaspoon bottled green hot pepper sauce**
- **1 tablespoon olive oil**
- **1 tablespoon lime juice**
- **¼ cup finely snipped fresh cilantro**
- **6 ounces peeled and cooked medium shrimp (12 to 15)**

1 In a bowl, combine tomatoes, tomatillos, tomato juice, cucumber, jalapeño, scallion, garlic, pepper sauce, oil, lime juice, and cilantro. Cover and chill for at least 1 hour.

2 To serve, reserve 6 shrimp. Coarsely chop remaining shrimp. Stir chopped shrimp into gazpacho. Spoon gazpacho into chilled bowls. Top with reserved whole shrimp.

Nutrition facts per serving: 90 cal., 3 g total fat (0 g sat. fat), 55 mg chol., 371 mg sodium, 10 g carb., 2 g dietary fiber, 8 g protein.

***Tip:** Because chile peppers contain volatile oils that can burn your skin and eyes, avoid direct contact with them as much as possible. When working with chile peppers, wear plastic or rubber gloves. If your bare hands do touch the peppers, wash your hands and nails well with soap and warm water.

jambalaya

Prep: 25 minutes
Cook: 20 minutes
Makes: 6 servings

1 **pound fresh or frozen peeled and deveined shrimp**

½ **cup chopped onion (1 medium)**

⅓ **cup chopped celery**

¼ **cup chopped green sweet pepper**

2 **cloves garlic, minced**

2 **tablespoons cooking oil**

2 **cups chicken broth**

1 **14.5-ounce can diced tomatoes, undrained**

8 **ounces andouille or kielbasa sausage, halved lengthwise and cut into ½-inch slices**

¾ **cup long grain rice**

1 **teaspoon dried thyme, crushed**

½ **teaspoon dried basil, crushed**

¼ **teaspoon ground black pepper**

¼ **teaspoon cayenne pepper**

1 **bay leaf**

1 **cup cubed cooked ham**

Thaw shrimp, if frozen. Rinse shrimp; pat dry with paper towels. In a 12-inch skillet, cook onion, celery, sweet pepper, and garlic in hot oil until tender. Stir in chicken broth, tomatoes, sausage, rice, thyme, basil, black pepper, red pepper, and bay leaf. Bring to boiling; reduce heat. Simmer, covered, for 15 minutes. Stir in shrimp. Return to boiling. Simmer, covered, for about 5 minutes more or until shrimp turn opaque and rice is tender. Stir in ham; heat through. Discard bay leaf.

Nutrition facts per serving: 416 cal., 20 g total fat (6 g sat. fat), 154 mg chol., 1199 mg sodium, 27 g carb., 1 g dietary fiber, 30 g protein.

creamy SHRIMP AND TOMATO CHOWDER

Start to Finish: 20 minutes
Makes: 4 servings

1 **8-ounce package frozen peeled and cooked large shrimp***

2 **stalks celery, chopped (1 cup)**

1 **medium onion, chopped (½ cup)**

1 **tablespoon olive oil**

2 **14.5-ounce cans diced tomatoes with garlic, basil, and oregano, undrained**

½ **cup whipping cream**

½ **cup water**

Ground black pepper

Finely shredded fresh basil

1 Thaw shrimp. Rinse shrimp; pat dry with paper towels. In a large saucepan, cook celery and onion in hot oil over medium heat just until tender. Stir in tomatoes; heat through.

2 Stir in shrimp, cream, and water. Cook over medium heat just until heated through, stirring occasionally. Season to taste with pepper. Sprinkle each serving with basil.

Nutrition facts per serving: 245 cal., 15 g total fat (8 g sat. fat), 152 mg chol., 1056 mg sodium, 14 g carb., 2 g dietary fiber, 15 g protein.

veggie FISH CHOWDER

Choose a firm-textured fish for this potato-based chowder, such as cod, salmon, halibut, or black sea bass.

Prep: 20 minutes
Cook: 10 minutes
Makes: 4 servings

1 pound cod, salmon, or other firm-textured fish, cut into 4 pieces

Ground black pepper

1 32-ounce carton reduced-sodium chicken broth

1 cup water

1 cup thinly sliced carrots (2 medium)

1 cup sugar snap peas, halved diagonally

1 4-ounce package (or ½ of a 7.2-ounce package) butter-and-herb-flavored instant mashed potatoes

¼ cup finely shredded Parmesan cheese

1 Season fish lightly with pepper. In a 4-quart pot, bring broth and water to boiling. Add carrots; cover and cook for 5 minutes. Add fish and peas. Return to boiling. Reduce heat. Simmer, covered, for 3 minutes or until fish flakes easily when tested with a fork.

2 Stir in mashed potatoes and simmer for 2 minutes.

3 Break fish into bite-size pieces. Ladle chowder into bowls. Sprinkle with Parmesan cheese.

Nutrition facts per serving: 269 cal., 5 g total fat (2 g sat. fat), 52 mg chol., 1269 mg sodium, 28 g carb., 3 g dietary fiber, 28 g protein.

manhattan CLAM CHOWDER

If you prefer, use purchased bacon pieces from a jar instead of regular bacon. Cook the celery, onion, and carrot in 2 tablespoons olive or cooking oil.

Start to Finish: 40 minutes
Makes: 4 servings

- **1 pint shucked clams, or two 6.5-ounce cans minced clams**
- **2 slices bacon**
- **1 cup chopped celery (2 stalks)**
- **¼ cup chopped carrot**
- **⅓ cup chopped onion (1 small)**
- **1 8-ounce bottle clam juice, or 1 cup chicken broth**
- **2 cups cubed red potatoes**
- **1 teaspoon dried thyme, crushed**
- **⅛ teaspoon cayenne pepper**
- **⅛ teaspoon ground black pepper**
- **1 14.5-ounce can diced tomatoes, undrained**

1 Chop fresh clams (if using), reserving juice; set clams aside. Strain clam juice to remove bits of shell. (Or, drain canned clams, reserving juice.) If necessary, add enough water to reserved clam juice to equal 1½ cups. Set juice aside.

2 In a large saucepan, cook bacon over medium heat until crisp. Remove bacon and drain on paper towels; crumble. Reserve 2 tablespoons drippings in pan.

3 Heat bacon drippings over medium heat. Add celery, carrot, and onion; cook and stir until tender. Stir in the reserved 1½ cups clam juice and the 8 ounces clam juice. Stir in potatoes, thyme, cayenne, and black pepper. Bring to boiling; reduce heat. Simmer, covered, for 10 minutes. Stir in clams, bacon, and tomatoes. Return to boiling; reduce heat. Cook for 1 to 2 minutes more or until heated through.

Nutrition facts per serving: 254 cal., 9 g total fat (1 g sat. fat), 41 mg chol., 507 mg sodium, 24 g carb., 3 g dietary fiber, 19 g protein.

clam CHOWDER

Prep: 25 minutes
Cook: 4½ to 5 hours (low)
or 2 to 2½ hours
(high)
Makes: 8 servings

3 **cups chopped celery
(6 stalks)**

1½ **cups chopped onions
(3 medium)**

1 **cup chopped carrots
(2 medium)**

2 **8-ounce bottles clam juice**

1 **14-ounce can reduced-
sodium chicken broth**

1½ **teaspoons dried thyme,
crushed**

½ **teaspoon salt**

½ **teaspoon coarsely ground
black pepper**

1 **cup fat-free half-and-half**

2 **tablespoons cornstarch**

2 **6.5-ounce cans chopped
clams, drained**

2 **tablespoons dry sherry
(optional)**

4 **slices turkey bacon,
crisp-cooked, drained,
and crumbled**

Sliced scallions (optional)

1 In a 3- to 4-quart slow cooker, combine celery, onions, carrots, clam juice, broth, thyme, salt, and pepper.

2 Cover and cook on low-heat setting for 4½ to 5 hours or on high-heat setting for 2 to 2½ hours.

3 If using low-heat setting, turn to high-heat setting. In a small bowl, combine half-and-half and cornstarch. Stir half-and-half mixture, clams, and (if desired) sherry into cooker. Cover and cook for 30 minutes more.

4 Sprinkle each serving with crumbled bacon and, if desired, scallions.

Nutrition facts per serving: 144 cal., 2 g total fat (0 g sat. fat), 38 mg chol., 309 mg sodium, 14 g carb., 2 g dietary fiber, 15 g protein.

north SEA CHOWDER

Prep: 15 minutes
Cook: 10 minutes
Makes: 4 to 6 servings

- 1 **pound fresh or frozen skinless, boneless sea bass, red snapper, and/or catfish fillets**
- 1 **medium onion, chopped**
- 1 **teaspoon bottled minced garlic (2 cloves)**
- 1 **tablespoon butter or olive oil**
- 4 **cups water**
- 1 **tablespoon lemon juice**
- 1 **bay leaf**
- 2 **fish bouillon cubes, or 2 teaspoons instant chicken bouillon granules**
- ½ **teaspoon instant chicken bouillon granules**
- ½ **teaspoon dried thyme, crushed**
- ¼ **teaspoon fennel seeds**
  Pinch of ground saffron (optional)
- 4 **roma tomatoes, halved lengthwise and thinly sliced**

1. Thaw fish, if frozen. Rinse fish; pat dry with paper towels. Cut fish into ¾-inch pieces; set aside.

2. In a large saucepan, cook onion and garlic in hot butter over medium heat until tender. Stir in the water, lemon juice, bay leaf, fish bouillon cubes, the ½ teaspoon chicken bouillon granules, thyme, fennel seeds, and (if desired) saffron. Bring to boiling.

3. Add fish and tomatoes. Return to boiling; reduce heat. Cover and simmer for about 10 minutes or until fish flakes easily with a fork, stirring once or twice. Discard bay leaf.

Nutrition facts per serving: 160 cal., 5 g total fat (2 g sat. fat), 55 mg chol., 683 mg sodium, 6 g carb., 1 g dietary fiber, 22 g protein.

smoked SALMON CHOWDER

This recipe takes chowder to another level. The smoked salmon provides a rich and smoky flavor that can be enjoyed as an appetizer to a Northwest-inspired meal. Or ladle a whole bowl for a cozy and warming soup supper.

Prep: 15 minutes
Cook: 25 minutes
Makes: 6 servings

¼ **cup butter**

2 **cups sliced leeks**

1 **clove garlic, minced**

2 **tablespoons all-purpose flour**

3 **cups fish stock or vegetable stock**

1½ **pounds yellow potatoes, peeled and cut into ¼-inch cubes (3 cups)**

1 **teaspoon salt**

¾ **pound smoked salmon, cut into bite-size pieces**

¾ **cup whipping cream**

Sliced leeks (optional)

Ground black pepper

1 In a 6-quart Dutch oven, melt butter over medium heat. Add the 2 cups leeks and garlic; cook and stir for 5 minutes or until soft. Stir in flour; cook and stir for 2 minutes more.

2 Gradually whisk the stock into the leek mixture in Dutch oven until smooth. Add potatoes and salt. Bring to boiling, stirring often. Reduce heat to medium. Simmer, covered, for 10 to 15 minutes or just until potatoes are tender. Stir in salmon and cream. Heat through. If desired, garnish each serving with additional sliced leeks. Sprinkle with pepper.

Nutrition facts per serving: 281 cal., 17 g total fat (9.6 g sat. fat), 58 mg chol., 845 mg sodium, 19 g carb., 2 g dietary fiber, 13 g protein.

mexican-style
FISH CHOWDER

Chunks of cod or other white fish get a flavor boost in this creamy, zesty chowder. It's one of those dishes that prove conclusively that fabulous food doesn't have to be complicated.

Prep: 15 minutes
Cook: 3 to 4 hours (low) or 1½ to 2 hours (high)
Makes: 6 to 8 servings

2　10.75-ounce cans condensed cream of celery soup

1　16-ounce package frozen whole kernel corn

1½　cups milk

1　pound fresh or frozen cod or other white fish fillets

2　14.5-ounce cans Mexican-style stewed tomatoes, undrained

1 Lightly coat the inside of a 3½- or 4-quart slow cooker with cooking spray. In the prepared cooker, combine soup, frozen corn, and milk.

2 Cover and cook on low-heat setting for 3 to 4 hours or on high-heat setting for 1½ to 2 hours.

3 Meanwhile, thaw fish, if frozen. Rinse fish; pat dry with paper towels. If using low-heat setting, turn to high-heat setting.

4 Stir corn mixture in cooker. Place fish on top of corn mixture. Cover and cook for 1 hour more. Stir in tomatoes and heat through.

Nutrition facts per serving: 293 cal., 8 g total fat (3 g sat. fat), 39 mg chol., 1296 mg sodium, 36 g carb., 2 g dietary fiber, 21 g protein.

shrimp AND CRAB GUMBO

Browning the flour gives the gumbo its distinctive rich color and flavor.

Prep: 30 minutes
Cook: 30 minutes
Makes: 8 servings

- 1 **pound fresh or frozen large shrimp in shells**
- ⅓ **cup all-purpose flour**
- 2 **tablespoons cooking oil**
- 2 **cups chopped onions**
- 1½ **cups chopped green or red sweet peppers**
- 4 **stalks celery, thinly sliced**
- 4 **cloves garlic, minced**
- 2 **14-ounce cans reduced-sodium beef broth**
- 1 **cup water**
  Cajun Spice Mix*
- 1 **16-ounce package frozen cut okra**
- 2 **6-ounce cans crabmeat, drained**
- 3 **cups hot cooked long grain rice or brown rice**
  Chopped scallions (optional)
  Bottled hot pepper sauce (optional)

1 Thaw shrimp, if frozen. Peel and devein shrimp, leaving tails intact if desired. Rinse shrimp; pat dry with paper towels. In a medium skillet, cook flour over medium heat for about 6 minutes or until flour is browned, stirring frequently. Place in a bowl; set aside to cool.

2 In a 4-quart Dutch oven, heat oil over medium-high heat. Add onions, sweet peppers, celery, and garlic; cook and stir about 5 minutes or until vegetables are tender.

3 Slowly whisk 1 can of the broth into browned flour. Add broth-flour mixture, remaining 1 can broth, the water, and Cajun Spice Mix to mixture in Dutch oven. Stir in okra. Bring to boiling; reduce heat. Cover and simmer for 15 minutes.

4 Add shrimp; cook for 2 to 3 minutes or until shrimp is opaque. Gently stir in crabmeat. Serve gumbo with rice. If desired, garnish individual servings with scallions. If desired, pass hot pepper sauce.

*Cajun Spice Mix: In a small bowl, combine ½ teaspoon dried thyme, crushed; ¼ teaspoon ground white pepper; ¼ teaspoon salt; ¼ teaspoon ground black pepper; and ¼ teaspoon crushed red pepper.

Nutrition facts per serving: 263 cal., 5 g total fat (1 g sat. fat), 102 mg chol., 510 mg sodium, 31 g carb., 4 g dietary fiber, 22 g protein.

simple SEAFOOD STEW

Prep: 40 minutes
Bake: 11 minutes
Oven: 450°F
Makes: 4 servings

1 pound fresh or frozen medium shrimp in shells and/or sea scallops

12 ounces fresh or frozen white fish fillets, such as cod, halibut, or flounder, cut into 2-inch pieces

1 tablespoon olive oil

⅓ cup chopped onion (1 small)

2 cloves garlic, thinly sliced

¼ teaspoon crushed red pepper

½ cup chopped tomato (1 medium)

¼ cup dry white wine

1 2-inch strip orange peel*

Pinch of saffron threads, or ⅛ teaspoon ground turmeric

2 8-ounce bottles clam juice

2 cups water

Salt and ground black pepper

4 thin slices crusty bread

Olive oil

1 clove garlic, halved

2 tablespoons finely snipped fresh parsley

1 Thaw seafood, if frozen. Peel and devein shrimp. Rinse seafood; pat dry with paper towels. Set aside. Preheat oven to 450°F.

2 In an ovenproof Dutch oven, heat the 1 tablespoon oil over medium heat. Add onion and sliced garlic; cook for about 4 minutes or until tender.

3 Add crushed red pepper; cook for 1 minute. Add tomato, wine, orange peel, and saffron; cook for 1 minute. Add clam juice and the water. Bring to boiling; remove from heat. Add seafood; sprinkle with salt and black pepper.

4 Bake, covered, for 6 to 8 minutes or until fish flakes easily when tested with a fork and shrimp and/or scallops are opaque.

5 Meanwhile, place bread slices on a baking sheet; drizzle with additional oil. Bake, uncovered, for 5 to 7 minutes or until bread is crisp and edges are golden brown. Rub surface of bread with cut sides of garlic halves.

6 Sprinkle each serving of stew with parsley. Serve with garlic-rubbed bread.

Nutrition facts per serving: 360 cal., 10 g total fat (2 g sat. fat), 209 mg chol., 788 mg sodium, 20 g carb., 2 g dietary fiber, 42 g protein.

*Tip: Use a vegetable peeler to remove a thin piece of peel from the orange. Be sure to get just the colored part, not the bitter white pith underneath.

caribbean FISH STEW

Ginger, jerk seasoning, lime, and garlic turn simple white fish into a tropical delight.

Prep: 30 minutes
Cook: 6 to 8 hours (low) or
      3 to 4 hours (high)
Makes: 6 servings

2   pounds sweet potatoes,
    peeled and coarsely
    chopped

1   large red sweet pepper,
    seeded and chopped

1   medium onion, chopped

1   tablespoon finely
    chopped fresh ginger

½   teaspoon grated lime zest

1   tablespoon lime juice

1   teaspoon Jamaican jerk
    seasoning

2   cloves garlic, minced

2   14-ounce cans chicken
    broth

1   14.5-ounce can diced
    tomatoes

1   pound firm white fish, cut
    into 1-inch pieces

2   tablespoons chopped
    fresh cilantro

1 In 4- to 5-quart slow cooker, combine sweet potatoes, sweet pepper, onion, ginger, lime zest, lime juice, jerk seasoning, and garlic. Pour chicken broth and tomatoes with their juices over.

2 Cover and cook on low-heat setting for 6 to 8 hours or on high-heat setting for 3 to 4 hours.

3 If necessary, raise temperature to high-heat setting. Stir in fish. Cover slow cooker; cook for about 15 minutes longer or until fish flakes easily when tested with a fork. Sprinkle each serving with cilantro.

Nutrition facts per serving: 232 cal., 5 g total fat (1 g sat. fat), 45 mg chol., 792 mg sodium, 29 g carb., 4 g dietary fiber, 17 g protein.

meatless

Broccoli-Potato Soup with Greens, *page 138*

vegetable SOUP WITH CORN BREAD CROUTONS

Prep: 40 minutes
Bake: 12 minutes
Oven: 350°F
Makes: 6 to 8 servings

- 1 tablespoon olive oil or vegetable oil
- ⅔ cup sliced leeks (2 medium), or ½ cup chopped onion (1 medium)
- 1 8-ounce package fresh mushrooms, quartered
- 1¼ cups coarsely chopped red or yellow sweet pepper (1 large)
- 4 cloves garlic, minced
- 3 cups water
- 1 28-ounce can whole Italian-style tomatoes, undrained, cut up
- 1 15- to 19-ounce can cannellini beans (white kidney beans), rinsed and drained
- 1 teaspoon sea salt, or ½ teaspoon salt
- ¼ teaspoon ground black pepper
- 4 cups baby spinach leaves
  Corn Bread Croutons* (optional)

1. In a 4-quart Dutch oven, heat oil over medium heat. Add leeks; cook until tender, stirring occasionally. Add mushrooms, sweet pepper, and garlic; cook for 5 minutes more, stirring occasionally.

2. Add the water, tomatoes, beans, salt, and black pepper. Bring to boiling; reduce heat. Simmer, uncovered, for 5 minutes.

3. Stir in spinach. If desired, serve with Corn Bread Croutons.

*Corn Bread Croutons: Preheat oven to 350°F. Grease a very large baking sheet or 2 large baking sheets. In a medium bowl, lightly beat 1 egg. Add one 8.5-ounce package corn muffin mix, ⅔ cup finely shredded Romano or Parmesan cheese, and 2 tablespoons milk. Drop by scant teaspoonfuls into small mounds onto prepared baking sheet(s). Lightly sprinkle with ground black pepper and, if desired, coarse sea salt. Bake for 12 to 14 minutes or until golden. Remove from baking sheet; cool completely on a wire rack. Transfer to an airtight container. Cover and seal. Store at room temperature for up to 1 day or in the refrigerator for up to 3 days. (Or place in a freezer container. Seal, label, and freeze for up to 1 month.) Let stand for 30 minutes at room temperature before serving. Makes about 28 croutons.

Nutrition facts per serving: 345 cal., 11 g total fat (2 g sat. fat), 42 mg chol., 933 mg sodium, 52 g carb., 6 g dietary fiber, 15 g protein.

barley-vegetable SOUP

Prep: 25 minutes
Cook: 8 to 10 hours (low)
      or 4 to 5 hours
      (high)
Makes: 6 servings

- 1 **cup chopped onion (1 large)**
- ½ **cup bias-sliced carrot (1 medium)**
- ½ **cup sliced celery (1 stalk)**
- 2 **cups sliced fresh mushrooms**
- 1 **15-ounce can red beans, rinsed and drained**
- 1 **14.5-ounce can stewed tomatoes**
- 1 **10-ounce package frozen whole kernel corn**
- ½ **cup regular barley (not quick-cooking)**
- 2 **teaspoons dried Italian seasoning, crushed**
- ¼ **teaspoon ground black pepper**
- 3 **cloves garlic, minced**
- 5 **cups vegetable or chicken broth**

1 In a 3½- to 5-quart slow cooker, place onion, carrot, and celery. Add mushrooms, red beans, undrained tomatoes, frozen corn, barley, Italian seasoning, pepper, and garlic. Pour broth over mushroom mixture in cooker.

2 Cover and cook on low-heat setting for 8 to 10 hours or on high-heat setting for 4 to 5 hours.

Nutrition facts per serving: 228 cal., 2 g total fat (0 g sat. fat), 0 mg chol., 1212 mg sodium, 47 g carb., 8 g dietary fiber, 9 g protein.

cheesy CAULIFLOWER, BROCCOLI, AND CORN SOUP

Dill takes the lead, lending its fragrance and flavor to a thick cheese soup. Slice some crisp apples to serve alongside each serving.

Prep: 20 minutes
Cook: 6 to 7 hours (low) or 3 to 3½ hours (high)
Makes: 8 to 10 servings

- 2 **10-ounce packages frozen cauliflower, thawed and well drained**
- 2 **10-ounce packages frozen cut broccoli, thawed and well drained**
- 1 **10-ounce package frozen whole kernel corn, thawed and well drained**
- 3 **14-ounce cans vegetable broth or chicken broth**
- 2 **teaspoons dried dill, crushed**
- 1 **pound American cheese, cut into cubes**

1 In a 5- to 6-quart slow cooker, combine cauliflower, broccoli, corn, broth, and dill.

2 Cover and cook on low-heat setting for 6 to 7 hours or on high-heat setting for 3 to 3½ hours.

3 If using the low-heat setting, turn to the high-heat setting. Stir cheese into cooker. Cover and cook for about 30 minutes more or until cheese is melted.

Nutrition facts per serving: 289 cal., 18 g total fat (11 g sat. fat), 52 mg chol., 1463 mg sodium, 17 g carb., 5 g dietary fiber, 17 g protein.

cream OF BROCCOLI SOUP

Serve this creamy soup with your favorite sandwich—lunch never tasted so good.

Start to Finish: 20 minutes
Makes: 6 to 8 servings

2 cups chopped broccoli

2 cups boiling water

3 tablespoons butter

¼ cup all-purpose flour

2 teaspoons instant chicken bouillon granules

2 cups half-and-half, light cream, or milk

Ground black pepper

1 In a large saucepan, cook the broccoli in the 2 cups boiling water for 8 to 10 minutes or until very tender. Drain broccoli, reserving cooking liquid. (Add additional water, if necessary, to make 1½ cups liquid.) In a blender, combine broccoli and the reserved cooking liquid. Cover and blend at low speed until smooth.

2 In the same saucepan, melt the butter. Stir in the flour and bouillon granules. Add half-and-half all at once. Cook and stir over medium heat until thickened and bubbly. Cook and stir for 1 minute more. Stir in broccoli mixture; heat through. Season to taste with pepper.

Nutrition facts per serving: 186 cal., 15 g total fat (10 g sat. fat), 46 mg chol., 393 mg sodium, 9 g carb., 1 g dietary fiber, 4 g protein.

minestrone

2 cloves garlic, minced

½ cup chopped onion
   (1 medium)

1 tablespoon olive oil

1 cup chopped yellow
   sweet pepper (1 large)

1¼ cups coarsely chopped
    zucchini (1 medium)

2 14-ounce cans beef broth

2 cups water

1 15-ounce cans cannellini
   beans, rinsed and drained

8 ounces green beans,
   trimmed and cut into
   1½-inch pieces

1 cup dried mostaccioli

¼ cup coarsely chopped
   fresh basil, or
   2 teaspoons dried
   basil, crushed

2 medium tomatoes, coarsely
   chopped, or 1½ cups
   cherry tomatoes, halved

2 cups packaged fresh baby
   spinach leaves

   Salt and ground black
   pepper

   Shaved Parmesan cheese
   (optional)

1 In a 5- to 6-quart Dutch oven, cook garlic and onion in hot oil until tender, stirring occasionally. Add sweet pepper, zucchini, beef broth, and water. Bring to boiling. Add beans, pasta, and dried basil (if using). Return to boiling; reduce heat. Simmer, covered, for 10 to 12 minutes or until pasta is tender, stirring occasionally.

2 Stir in tomatoes, spinach, and fresh basil (if using). Remove from heat. Season to taste with salt and black pepper. If desired, top with Parmesan cheese.

Nutrition facts per serving: 182 cal., 3 g total fat (0 g sat. fat), 0 mg chol., 717 mg sodium, 33 g carb., 7 g dietary fiber, 10 g protein.

avocado SOUP

This elegant first-course soup is sublime. Blend the ingredients until they're almost but not quite smooth, with a bit of texture remaining from the onion and carrot.

Prep: 20 minutes
Chill: 1 hour
Makes: 6 appetizer
        servings

- 2 **medium ripe avocados, pitted, peeled, and cut up**
- ½ **cup peeled and chopped cucumber**
- ⅓ **cup chopped onion (1 small)**
- ¼ **cup shredded carrot**
- 1 **clove garlic, minced**
- 2 **14-ounce cans reduced-sodium chicken broth**
- **Several dashes of bottled hot pepper sauce**
- 1½ **teaspoons paprika**
- ⅓ **cup bottled salsa (optional)**

1 In a blender or food processor, combine avocados, cucumber, onion, carrot, garlic, and 1 can of the chicken broth. Cover and blend or process until almost smooth.

2 Add remaining chicken broth and bottled hot pepper sauce. Cover and blend or process until smooth. Pour soup into a bowl. Cover surface with plastic wrap and chill for 1 to 24 hours.

3 To serve, ladle soup into chilled soup cups. Sprinkle each serving with paprika. If desired, top with salsa.

Nutrition facts per serving: 92 cal., 7 g total fat (1 g sat. fat), 0 mg chol., 322 mg sodium, 6 g carb., 4 g dietary fiber, 3 g protein.

tomato-tortellini SOUP

Start to Finish: 15 minutes
Makes: 4 servings

2 **14-ounce cans reduced-sodium chicken broth or vegetable broth**

1 **9-ounce package refrigerated tortellini**

½ **of an 8-ounce tub cream cheese spread with chive and onion**

1 **10.75- or 11-ounce can condensed tomato or tomato bisque soup**

Snipped fresh chives (optional)

In a medium saucepan, bring broth to boiling. Add tortellini; reduce heat. Simmer, uncovered, for 5 minutes. In a bowl, whisk ⅓ cup of the hot broth into the cream cheese spread until smooth. Return all to saucepan along with tomato soup; heat through. Sprinkle with chives before serving.

Nutrition facts per serving: 363 cal., 14 g total fat (8 g sat. fat), 57 mg chol., 1264 mg sodium, 44 g carb., 1 g dietary fiber, 14 g protein.

broccoli-potato SOUP WITH GREENS

Start to Finish: 20 minutes
Makes: 4 servings

2 **medium red potatoes, chopped**

1 **14-ounce can reduced-sodium chicken broth**

3 **cups small broccoli florets**

2 **cups milk**

3 **tablespoons all-purpose flour**

2 **cups smoked Gouda cheese, shredded (8 ounces)**

   Ground black pepper

2 **cups winter greens (such as curly endive, chicory, romaine, escarole, or spinach)**

   Gouda cheese, shredded (optional)

① In a large saucepan, combine potatoes and broth. Bring to boiling; reduce heat. Simmer, covered, for 8 minutes. Mash slightly. Add broccoli and milk; bring just to simmering.

② In a medium bowl, toss flour with cheese; gradually add to soup, stirring cheese until melted. Season to taste with black pepper. Divide among shallow serving bowls. Top with greens and additional cheese.

Nutrition facts per serving: 365 cal., 18 g total fat (11 g sat. fat), 74 mg chol., 782 mg sodium, 28 g carb., 4 g dietary fiber, 23 g protein.

baked-potato SOUP

This soup, which tastes like a baked potato in a bowl, is the perfect side dish for sandwiches or a chef's salad.

Start to Finish: 1 hour
Oven: 425°F
Makes: 6 to 8 servings

- **4 medium baking potatoes (about 1⅓ pounds total)**
- **¼ cup butter**
- **¼ cup all-purpose flour**
- **¼ teaspoon ground white pepper**
- **4 cups chicken broth**
- **1½ cups whipping cream**
- **⅓ cup sour cream**
- **1 tablespoon snipped chives or thinly sliced scallion tops**

1. Preheat oven to 425°F. Scrub potatoes with a brush. Pat dry with paper towels. Prick potatoes thoroughly with a fork. Bake for 40 to 60 minutes or until tender.* Cool potatoes. Scoop out into a bowl, discarding skins. Mash potatoes.

2. In a large saucepan, melt butter. Stir in flour and pepper until smooth. Add mashed potatoes; stir in chicken broth. Cook and stir until thickened and bubbly. Cook and stir for 1 minute more.

3. Stir in whipping cream, sour cream, and chives. Heat through, but don't boil. (For a thinner consistency, stir in a little additional chicken broth.)

Nutrition facts per serving: 389 cal., 33 g total fat (19 g sat. fat), 110 mg chol., 744 mg sodium, 20 g carb., 1 g dietary fiber, 5 g protein.

*Tip: To microcook potatoes, prick potatoes with a fork. On a microwave-safe plate, arrange potatoes, spoke fashion. Microcook, uncovered, on 100% power for 10 to 15 minutes or until tender, rearranging and turning potatoes over once. Continue as directed.

sweet potato SOUP WITH NUTMEG AND MAPLE SYRUP

This soup has a sweet taste that everyone will find appealing. Use pure maple syrup for the best flavor.

Prep: 20 minutes
Cook: 20 minutes
Makes: 4 servings

½ **cup chopped onion (1 medium)**

½ **cup chopped celery (1 stalk)**

1 **clove garlic, minced**

1 **tablespoon butter**

1 **sweet potato, peeled and cubed (about 2 cups)**

2 **cups reduced-sodium chicken broth**

½ **teaspoon ground nutmeg**

1½ **cups half-and-half or light cream**

1 **tablespoon maple syrup**

Sour cream (optional)

Ground nutmeg (optional)

1 In a 4-quart Dutch oven, cook onion, celery, and garlic in hot butter over medium heat until onion is tender but not brown. Add sweet potato, broth, and the ½ teaspoon nutmeg; bring to boiling. Reduce heat and simmer, covered, for 20 minutes or until potato is tender. Remove from heat; cool slightly.

2 Transfer mixture, about one-third at a time, to a blender or food processor. Cover and blend or process until smooth. Return all soup to the Dutch oven. Stir in half-and-half and maple syrup; heat through. If desired, top each serving with sour cream and additional nutmeg.

Nutrition facts per serving: 233 cal., 13 g total fat (8 g sat. fat), 41 mg chol., 392 mg sodium, 24 g carb., 3 g dietary fiber, 6 g protein.

french ONION SOUP

Fit this classic French dish into your schedule by cooking it for as little as 2½ hours or as long as 10 hours.

Prep: 30 minutes
Cook: 5 to 10 hours (low)
      or 2½ to 3 hours
      (high)
Makes: 6 servings

- 4 to 6 onions, thinly sliced (4 to 6 cups)
- 1 clove garlic, minced
- 3 tablespoons butter or margarine
- 4½ cups beef broth
- 1½ teaspoons Worcestershire sauce
- ⅛ teaspoon ground black pepper
- 6 1-inch slices baguette-style bread (optional)
- ½ cup shredded Swiss or Gruyère cheese

1 In a large skillet, cook onions and garlic in hot butter, covered, over medium-low heat for about 20 minutes or until tender, stirring occasionally.

2 Transfer onion mixture to a 3½- or 4-quart slow cooker. Add beef broth, Worcestershire sauce, and pepper. Cover and cook on low-heat setting for 5 to 10 hours or on high-heat setting for 2½ to 3 hours.

3 Ladle soup into bowls. If desired, place a slice of bread on each serving. Sprinkle with cheese.

Nutrition facts per serving: 126 cal., 9 g total fat (6 g sat. fat), 25 mg chol., 719 mg sodium, 6 g carb., 1 g dietary fiber, 5 g protein.

tofu-carrot SOUP

Prep: 30 minutes
Cook: 25 minutes
Makes: 6 servings

1 8-ounce package sliced fresh button mushrooms (2½ cups)

2 stalks celery, sliced

1 medium onion, sliced

2 cloves garlic, minced

2 tablespoons vegetable oil

4 cups sliced carrots

3 14-ounce cans vegetable broth or chicken broth

1 12.3-ounce package silken-style firm tofu, cut up

1 5-ounce can evaporated milk

1 teaspoon chopped fresh thyme

Salt and ground black pepper

½ cup sour cream

Fresh thyme (optional)

Cayenne pepper (optional)

1 In 4- to 6- quart Dutch oven, cook mushrooms, celery, onion, and garlic in hot oil over medium heat for 5 minutes or until softened. Add carrots and broth to mixture. Bring to boiling; reduce heat. Simmer, covered, for 20 minutes or until tender.

2 Let soup cool slightly. Place the tofu and half of the broth mixture in a large food processor or blender. (If you don't have a large food processor or blender, process mixture in smaller batches.) Cover and process or blend until smooth. Repeat with remaining broth mixture and evaporated milk. Cover and process or blend until smooth. Return all blended soup to Dutch oven and heat through. Stir in the 1 teaspoon thyme and salt and pepper to taste. Top servings with sour cream thinned with 2 to 3 teaspoons water, snipped thyme, and pepper.

Nutrition facts per serving: 205 cal., 11 g total fat (4 g sat. fat), 15 mg chol., 1003 mg sodium, 18 g carb., 3 g dietary fiber, 8 g protein.

egg DROP SOUP

Prep: 15 minutes
Bake: 6 minutes
Cook: 10 minutes
Oven: 375°F
Makes: 4 servings

Nonstick cooking spray

1 **egg roll wrapper, cut into ¼-inch-wide strips**

6 **cups reduced-sodium chicken broth**

4 **teaspoons reduced-sodium soy sauce**

1 **clove garlic, minced**

¼ **teaspoon ground white pepper**

2 **medium carrots**

½ **cup frozen baby peas**

8 **teaspoons cornstarch**

4 **eggs**

2 **scallions, bias-sliced**

1 Preheat oven to 375°F. Lightly coat a baking sheet with cooking spray. Place egg roll strips on prepared baking sheet. Lightly coat egg roll strips with cooking spray. Bake for 6 to 7 minutes or until light brown and crisp, stirring halfway through baking; set aside.

2 In a large saucepan, combine 5 cups of the broth, the soy sauce, garlic, and white pepper. Bring to boiling.

3 To make carrot flowers, peel carrots; with a paring knife or channel knife,* make 4 or 5 shallow lengthwise notches around the circumference of the carrot before thinly slicing. (Or, thinly slice carrots; cut each with a 1-inch or smaller flower-shaped cutter.) Add carrots and peas to boiling broth and return to boiling.

4 Stir cornstarch into remaining 1 cup broth; stir into soup. Reduce heat. Cook and stir until slightly thickened and bubbly; cook and stir for 2 minutes more.

5 Remove from heat. In a liquid measuring cup, use a fork to beat eggs. While gently stirring the broth, pour eggs in a thin stream into soup to form fine shreds. Ladle soup into bowls. Garnish with scallions. Serve with egg roll crisps.

Nutrition facts per serving: 186 cal., 5 g total fat (2 g sat. fat), 212 mg chol., 559 mg sodium, 18 g carb., 2 g dietary fiber, 15 g protein.

*Tip: A channel knife is a garnishing tool used to make thin strips of citrus peel and other garnishes.

hearty GARLIC AND SNAP PEA SOUP

Start to Finish: 30 minutes
Makes: 8 appetizer
servings

1 **medium fennel bulb**

2 **tablespoons olive oil**

4 **cloves garlic, minced, or
1 to 2 bulbs spring
garlic, chopped**

¼ **cup chopped onion**

2 **14-ounce cans reduced-
sodium chicken broth**

1 **pound Yukon gold
potatoes, quartered**

1¾ **cups water**

1½ **cups sugar snap peas,
trimmed**

½ **teaspoon salt**

¼ **teaspoon ground black
pepper**

Plain yogurt (optional)

Olive oil (optional)

1 Trim tough stalks and bottom stem from fennel bulb; reserve leafy tops. Cut the bulb and tender stalks into thin slivers. Snip enough leafy tops to measure 1 tablespoon; discard remaining tops. Set aside.

2 In a large saucepan, heat the 2 tablespoons oil over medium heat. Add garlic; cook for 1 minute. Add onion and cook until tender. Add broth, potatoes, and the water. Bring to boiling; reduce heat. Cover and cook for 15 to 18 minutes or until potatoes are tender. Cool slightly.

3 Place one-third of the potato mixture in a blender or food processor. Cover and blend or process until smooth. Transfer to a bowl. Repeat two more times with the remaining potato mixture. Return all of the potato mixture to saucepan. Add slivered fennel and sugar snap peas. Bring to boiling; reduce heat. Simmer, uncovered, for 3 minutes.

4 Stir in salt and pepper. If desired, spoon yogurt onto each serving and drizzle with additional oil. Top each serving with fennel tops.

Nutrition facts per serving: 102 cal., 3 g total fat (0 g sat. fat), 0 mg chol., 403 mg sodium, 15 g carb., 3 g dietary fiber, 3 g protein.

creamy TORTELLINI SOUP

White sauce mix and dried tortellini make this satisfying soup extra-easy; stirring in the spinach at the last minute gives it fresh-from-the-garden flavor.

Prep: 20 minutes
Cook: 5 to 6 hours (low)
or 2½ to 3 hours
(high)
Makes: 4 servings

- 1 **1.8-ounce envelope white sauce mix**
- 4 **cups water**
- 1 **14-ounce can vegetable broth**
- 1½ **cups sliced fresh mushrooms**
- ½ **cup chopped onion**
- 3 **cloves garlic, minced**
- ½ **teaspoon dried basil, crushed**
- ¼ **teaspoon salt**
- ¼ **teaspoon dried oregano, crushed**
- ⅛ **teaspoon cayenne pepper**
- 1 **7- to 8-ounce package dried cheese tortellini (about 2 cups)**
- 1 **12-ounce can evaporated milk**
- 6 **cups baby spinach leaves or torn spinach**
  Ground black pepper (optional)
  Finely shredded Parmesan cheese (optional)

1 Place dry white sauce mix in a 3½- or 4-quart slow cooker. Gradually add the water to the white sauce mix, stirring until smooth. Stir in broth, mushrooms, onion, garlic, basil, salt, oregano, and cayenne.

2 Cover and cook on low-heat setting for 5 to 6 hours or on high-heat setting for 2½ to 3 hours.

3 Stir in dried tortellini. Cover and cook on low-heat setting for 1 hour more or high-heat setting for 45 minutes more.

4 Stir in evaporated milk and spinach. If desired, sprinkle individual servings with black pepper and Parmesan cheese.

Nutrition facts per serving: 450 cal., 18 g total fat (7 g sat. fat), 34 mg chol., 1710 mg sodium, 53 g carb., 2 g dietary fiber, 22 g protein.

italian BEAN AND PASTA SOUP

Start to Finish: 30 minutes
Makes: 6 servings

- 1 **large onion, chopped (1 cup)**
- 1 **teaspoon bottled minced garlic**
- 1 **tablespoon olive oil**
- 2 **14-ounce cans vegetable broth**
- 1 **medium green sweet pepper, seeded and chopped**
- ½ **cup dried orzo**
- 2 **14.5-ounce cans diced tomatoes with garlic, basil, and oregano, undrained**
- 1 **19-ounce can fava beans, rinsed and drained**
- 1 **15-ounce can navy beans, rinsed and drained**
- ¼ **cup snipped fresh Italian (flat-leaf) parsley**

1 In 4- to 5-quart Dutch oven, cook onion and garlic in hot oil over medium heat for 5 minutes or until tender, stirring occasionally. Add broth; bring to boiling.

2 Add sweet pepper and orzo. Return to boiling; reduce heat. Simmer, uncovered, for 8 to 10 minutes or until orzo is tender. Stir in tomatoes, fava beans, and navy beans. Cover and simmer for 5 minutes. Stir in parsley.

Nutrition facts per serving: 295 cal., 3 g total fat (0 g sat. fat), 0 mg chol., 1953 mg sodium, 54 g carb., 9 g dietary fiber, 15 g protein.

hearty BLACK BEAN SOUP

Start to Finish: 30 minutes
Makes: 6 servings

2 **14-ounce cans vegetable broth**

2 **15-ounce cans black beans, rinsed and drained**

1 **14.5-ounce can diced tomatoes and green chiles, undrained**

1 **11-ounce can whole kernel corn with sweet peppers, drained**

1 **teaspoon ground cumin**

Sour cream (optional)

Shredded cheddar cheese (optional)

In a large saucepan, combine broth, beans, tomatoes, corn, and cumin. Bring to boiling; reduce heat. Simmer, covered, for 10 minutes. Ladle soup into bowls. If desired, garnish each serving with sour cream and shredded cheese.

Nutrition facts per serving: 155 cal., 1 g total fat (0 g sat. fat), 0 mg chol., 1348 mg sodium, 33 g carb., 9 g dietary fiber, 11 g protein.

pumpkin-bean SOUP

Start to Finish: 15 minutes
Makes: 4 servings

1 **15-ounce can pumpkin**

1 **15-ounce can cannellini (white kidney) beans, rinsed and drained**

1 **14-ounce can unsweetened coconut milk**

1 **14-ounce can vegetable broth**

1 **teaspoon dried sage, crushed**

Salt and cracked black pepper

Fresh lime wedges (optional)

1 In a medium saucepan, combine pumpkin, beans, coconut milk, broth, and sage. Heat through. Season with salt.

2 Ladle soup into bowls. Sprinkle with pepper. If desired, serve with lime wedges.

Nutrition facts per serving: 285 cal., 19 g total fat (17 g sat. fat), 0 mg chol., 729 mg sodium, 28 g carb., 8 g dietary fiber, 9 g protein.

southwestern BEAN SOUP

Prep: 25 minutes
Cook: 10 to 12 hours
(low) or 5 to
6 hours (high)
Makes: 6 servings

3 cups water

1 15-ounce can red kidney beans, rinsed and drained

1 15-ounce can black beans, pinto beans, or Great Northern beans, rinsed and drained

1 14.5-ounce can Mexican-style stewed tomatoes, undrained

1 10-ounce package frozen whole kernel corn

1 cup sliced carrots

1 large onion, chopped

1 4-ounce can diced green chile peppers

2 tablespoons instant beef or chicken bouillon granules

1 to 2 teaspoons chili powder

2 cloves garlic, minced

⅓ cup all-purpose flour

¼ cup yellow cornmeal

1 teaspoon baking powder

Ground black pepper

1 egg white

2 tablespoons milk

1 tablespoon cooking oil

1 In a 3½- or 4-quart slow cooker, combine the water, beans, tomatoes, corn, carrots, onion, undrained chile peppers, bouillon granules, chili powder, and garlic.

2 Cover and cook for on low-heat setting for 10 to 12 hours or on high-heat setting for 5 to 6 hours.

3 For dumplings, in a medium bowl, stir together flour, cornmeal, baking powder, and black pepper. In a small bowl, whisk together egg white, milk, and oil. Add to flour mixture; stir with a fork just until combined.

4 Drop dumpling dough into 6 mounds on top of the bubbling soup. Cover and cook on low-heat setting for about 30 minutes more or on high-heat setting for about 20 minutes more or until a toothpick inserted in center of a dumpling comes out clean. (Do not lift lid while dumplings are cooking.)

Nutrition facts per serving: 263 cal., 4 g total fat (1 g sat. fat), 1 mg chol., 1434 mg sodium, 51 g carb., 11 g dietary fiber, 15 g protein.

curried LENTIL SOUP

Fresh ginger, curry powder, and a jalapeño chile season this hearty, meatless soup.

Prep: 20 minutes
Cook: 8 to 10 hours (low)
　　　or 4 to 5 hours
　　　(high)
Makes: 4 to 6 servings

2　medium sweet potatoes (about 1 pound), peeled and coarsely chopped

1　cup dried brown or yellow lentils, rinsed and drained

1　medium onion, chopped

1　medium fresh jalapeño chile, seeded and finely chopped*

3　cloves garlic, chopped

3　14-ounce cans vegetable broth

1　14.5-ounce can diced tomatoes

1　tablespoon curry powder

1　teaspoon finely chopped fresh ginger

　　Plain yogurt or sour cream (optional)

　　Small fresh chiles and/or crushed red pepper (optional)

1 In 4- to 5-quart slow cooker, combine sweet potatoes, lentils, onion, jalapeño, and garlic. Add vegetable broth, undrained tomatoes, curry powder, and ginger.

2 Cover and cook on low-heat setting for 8 to 10 hours or on high-heat setting for 4 to 5 hours. If desired, top each serving with yogurt and garnish with chiles and/or crushed red pepper.

Nutrition facts per serving: 316 cal., 2 g total fat (0 g sat. fat), 0 mg chol., 1425 mg sodium, 60 g carb., 18 g dietary fiber, 18 g protein.

*Tip: Because chiles contain volatile oils that can burn your skin and eyes, avoid direct contact with them as much as possible. When working with chiles, wear plastic or rubber gloves. If your bare hands do touch the chiles, wash your hands and nails well with soap and warm water.

lentil SOUP WITH BROWN RICE

This warming soup is deliciously topped with a sprinkling of Asiago cheese, which gives it a rich, nutty flavor.

Prep: 25 minutes
Cook: 40 minutes
Makes: 6 servings

- 3 tablespoons olive oil
- 1 cup chopped onion (1 large)
- 1 cup chopped celery (2 stalks)
- 6 cloves garlic, minced
- 8 cups reduced-sodium chicken broth or chicken stock
- ½ cup long grain brown rice
- 2 cups chopped tomatoes (4 medium)
- ¾ cup dried brown lentils, rinsed and drained
- 1 tablespoon snipped fresh thyme
- 1 tablespoon snipped fresh oregano
- 1 tablespoon lemon juice
- ¼ teaspoon ground black pepper
- 2 tablespoons finely shredded Asiago cheese
- Fresh thyme sprigs and/or oregano leaves

1 In a 4-quart Dutch oven, heat oil over medium heat. Add onion, celery, and garlic; cook for about 5 minutes or until tender, stirring occasionally. Stir in broth and brown rice. Bring to boiling; reduce heat. Simmer, uncovered, for 10 minutes. Stir in tomatoes and lentils. Return to boiling; reduce heat. Cover and simmer for about 30 minutes more or until rice and lentils are tender.

2 Stir in snipped thyme, snipped oregano, lemon juice, and pepper. Top each serving with Asiago cheese. If desired, garnish with thyme sprigs and/or oregano leaves.

Nutrition facts per serving: 257 cal., 9 g total fat (2 g sat. fat), 3 mg chol., 810 mg sodium, 34 g carb., 9 g dietary fiber, 14 g protein.

garbanzo BEAN STEW

Garbanzo beans are one of those wonderfully rich and hearty legumes that make it easy to go meatless now and then, especially when you pair them with potatoes and just the right spices.

Prep: 25 minutes
Cook: 9 to 10 hours (low)
or 4½ to 5 hours
(high)
Makes: 8 servings

3 15-ounce cans garbanzo beans (chickpeas), rinsed and drained

1 pound red-skin potatoes, cut into ¾-inch pieces

1 14.5-ounce can no-salt-added diced tomatoes

¾ cup chopped red sweet pepper (1 medium)

½ cup chopped onion (1 medium)

3 cloves garlic, minced

2 teaspoons cumin seeds, toasted

½ teaspoon paprika

¼ teaspoon cayenne pepper

2¼ cups water

1¼ cups vegetable broth

1 In a 5- to 6-quart slow cooker, stir together garbanzo beans, potatoes, undrained tomatoes, sweet pepper, onion, garlic, 1 teaspoon of the cumin seeds, paprika, and cayenne. Pour the water and broth over bean mixture in cooker.

2 Cover and cook on low-heat setting for 9 to 10 hours or on high-heat setting for 4½ to 5 hours. Sprinkle each serving with some of the remaining cumin seeds.

Nutrition facts per serving: 258 cal., 2 g total fat (0 g sat. fat), 0 mg chol., 652 mg sodium, 51 g carb., 10 g dietary fiber, 10 g protein.

tuscan RAVIOLI STEW

Broccoli rabe, a leafy green with stalks and broccoli-like buds that is popular in Italian cuisine, has a pungent, somewhat bitter flavor. If it's not available, substitute broccoli florets.

Start to Finish: 30 minutes
Makes: 4 servings

- 1 tablespoon olive oil
- ⅓ cup sliced leek (1 medium)
- 1½ teaspoons bottled minced garlic (3 cloves)
- 1 14-ounce can vegetable broth or beef broth
- ¾ cup water
- ¼ teaspoon crushed red pepper (optional)
- 5 cups coarsely chopped broccoli rabe or broccoli florets
- 1 14.5-ounce can no-salt-added stewed tomatoes, undrained
- 1 9-ounce package refrigerated cheese-filled ravioli
- 1 tablespoon snipped fresh rosemary, or 1 teaspoon dried rosemary, crushed
- ¼ cup grated Asiago or Parmesan cheese (optional)

1. In a large saucepan, heat oil over medium heat. Add leek and garlic; cook for 5 minutes. Add broth, the water, and (if desired) crushed red pepper. Bring to boiling.

2. Add broccoli rabe, tomatoes, ravioli, and rosemary. Return to boiling; reduce heat. Cover and simmer for 7 to 8 minutes or until broccoli rabe and ravioli are tender. If desired, sprinkle each serving with cheese.

Nutrition facts per serving: 363 cal., 16 g total fat (9 g sat. fat), 55 mg chol., 995 mg sodium, 41 g carb., 5 g dietary fiber, 13 g protein.

chili

All-American Chili, *page 173*

chicken FAJITA CHILI

Combine the ingredients in your slow cooker before you head out the door to run errands. Supper will be ready when you return.

Prep: 20 minutes
Cook: 4 to 5 hours (low)
or 2 to 2½ hours
(high)
Makes: 6 servings

- 2 **pounds skinless, boneless chicken breast halves, cut into 1-inch pieces**
- 1 **tablespoon chili powder**
- 1 **teaspoon fajita seasoning**
- 2 **cloves garlic, minced**
- ½ **teaspoon ground cumin**
- 2 **14.5-ounce cans no-salt-added diced tomatoes, undrained**
- 1 **16-ounce package frozen sweet pepper and onion stir-fry vegetables**
- 1 **15-ounce can cannellini beans (white kidney beans), rinsed and drained**
- 3 **tablespoons shredded reduced-fat cheddar cheese (optional)**
- 3 **tablespoons light sour cream (optional)**
- 3 **tablespoons guacamole (optional)**

1 In a medium bowl, combine chicken, chili powder, fajita seasoning, garlic, and cumin; toss gently to coat. Coat a large skillet with cooking spray; heat skillet over medium-high heat. Cook chicken, half at a time, in hot skillet until browned, stirring occasionally.

2 Transfer chicken to a 3½- or 4-quart slow cooker. Stir in tomatoes, frozen vegetables, and beans. Cover and cook on low-heat setting for 4 to 5 hours or on high-heat setting for 2 to 2½ hours.

3 If desired, top each serving with cheese, sour cream, and guacamole.

Nutrition facts per serving: 261 cal., 2 g total fat (1 g sat. fat), 88 mg chol., 294 mg sodium, 22 g carb., 7 g dietary fiber, 41 g protein.

chicken SALSA CHILI

Prep: 15 minutes
Cook: 20 minutes
Makes: 6 servings

1 16-ounce jar chunky salsa

1 15-ounce can yellow hominy or garbanzo beans (chickpeas), rinsed and drained

1 15-ounce can dark red kidney beans or black beans, rinsed and drained

1 14-ounce can chicken broth

1 9-ounce package frozen diced cooked chicken

1 4-ounce can diced green chile peppers, undrained

1 tablespoon chili powder

2 teaspoons bottled minced garlic (4 cloves), or ½ teaspoon garlic powder

¼ to ½ teaspoon crushed red pepper

¼ cup snipped fresh cilantro

2 tablespoons lime juice

Chopped red onion and/or sliced scallion (optional)

Shredded sharp cheddar cheese (optional)

Chopped avocado (optional)

Sour cream or plain low-fat yogurt (optional)

1 In a 4-quart Dutch oven, combine salsa, hominy, beans, broth, chicken, chile peppers, chili powder, garlic, and crushed red pepper. Bring to boiling; reduce heat. Cover and simmer for 20 minutes.

2 Just before serving, stir in cilantro and lime juice. If desired, top each serving with red onion, cheese, avocado, and/or sour cream.

Nutrition facts per serving: 190 cal., 2 g total fat (0 g sat. fat), 23 mg chol., 1200 mg sodium, 27 g carb., 7 g dietary fiber, 17 g protein.

southwestern WHITE CHILI

White chili differs from traditional chili in that it uses chicken instead of beef, white beans instead of red, and chicken broth instead of tomatoes.

Prep: 20 minutes
Cook: 8 to 10 hours (low)
 or 4 to 5 hours
 (high)
Makes: 8 servings

3 **15.5-ounce cans Great Northern beans, rinsed and drained**

4 **cups reduced-sodium chicken broth**

3 **cups chopped cooked chicken (about 15 ounces)**

2 **4-ounce cans diced green chile peppers, undrained**

1 **cup chopped onion (1 large)**

4 **cloves garlic, minced**

2 **teaspoons ground cumin**

1 **teaspoon dried oregano, crushed**

¼ **teaspoon cayenne pepper**

2 **cups shredded Monterey Jack cheese (8 ounces)**

Sour cream (optional)

Fresh cilantro leaves (optional)

1 In a 3½- to 5-quart slow cooker, combine beans, broth, chicken, chile peppers, onion, garlic, cumin, oregano, and cayenne pepper.

2 Cover and cook on low-heat setting for 8 to 10 hours or on high-heat setting for 4 to 5 hours.

3 Add cheese; stir until melted. If desired, top each serving with sour cream and cilantro.

Nutrition facts per serving: 429 cal., 14 g total fat (7 g sat. fat), 72 mg chol., 570 mg sodium, 41 g carb., 9 g dietary fiber, 37 g protein.

turkey–wild rice CHILI

Prep: 20 minutes
Cook: 7 to 8 hours (low)
or 3½ to 4 hours
(high)
Makes: 8 servings

1 **pound skinless, boneless turkey or chicken breast, cut into ½-inch pieces**

1 **15.25-ounce can whole kernel corn, drained**

1 **15-ounce can Great Northern beans, rinsed and drained**

⅔ **cup wild rice, rinsed and drained**

2 **4.5-ounce cans diced green chile peppers, undrained**

1 **medium onion, chopped**

1 **tablespoon chili powder**

1 **teaspoon ground cumin**

1 **teaspoon bottled minced garlic (2 cloves)**

Few dashes of bottled hot pepper sauce

2 **14-ounce cans chicken broth**

1¼ **cups water**

½ **cup shredded Monterey Jack cheese**

½ **cup sour cream**

Snipped fresh parsley (optional)

1 In 4- to 5-quart slow cooker, combine turkey, corn, beans, wild rice, green chile peppers, onion, chili powder, cumin, garlic, and hot pepper sauce. Stir in the broth and water.

2 Cover and cook on low-heat setting for 7 to 8 hours or on high-heat setting for 3½ to 4 hours. Top each serving with Monterey Jack cheese and sour cream. If desired, sprinkle with parsley.

Nutrition facts per serving: 303 cal., 9 g total fat (5 g sat. fat), 53 mg chol., 676 mg sodium, 32 g carb., 5 g dietary fiber, 25 g protein.

new WORLD CHILI

Prep: 25 minutes
Cook: 10 to 12 hours
(low) or 5 to
6 hours (high)
Makes: 6 servings

1 **pound turkey breast tenderloin, cut into 1-inch pieces**

1 **28-ounce can diced tomatoes, undrained**

1 **15-ounce can black beans, rinsed and drained**

1 **8-ounce can tomato sauce**

1 **cup peeled, seeded, and cubed butternut squash or pumpkin**

½ **cup chopped onion (1 medium)**

½ **cup chicken broth**

½ **cup frozen whole kernel corn**

½ **cup dried cranberries**

1 **fresh jalapeño chile pepper, seeded and finely chopped***

1 **tablespoon chili powder**

1 **clove garlic, minced**

Chicken broth (optional)

2 **cups shredded spinach**

4 **ounces Monterey Jack cheese with jalapeño chile peppers, shredded (1 cup)**

① In a 5-quart slow cooker, combine turkey, tomatoes, beans, tomato sauce, squash, onion, the ½ cup broth, the corn, cranberries, jalapeño, chili powder, and garlic.

② Cover and cook on low-heat setting for 10 to 12 hours or on high-heat setting for 5 to 6 hours. If desired, stir in additional broth to reach desired consistency. Stir in spinach just before serving. Sprinkle each serving with cheese.

Nutrition facts per serving: 301 cal., 7 g total fat (4 g sat. fat), 64 mg chol., 1051 mg sodium, 35 g carb., 8 g dietary fiber, 29 g protein.

*Tip: Because chile peppers contain volatile oils that can burn your skin and eyes, avoid direct contact with them as much as possible. When working with chile peppers, wear plastic or rubber gloves. If your bare hands do touch the peppers, wash your hands and nails well with soap and warm water.

turkey and white bean
CHILI WITH CORNBREAD DUMPLINGS

Start to Finish: 25 minutes
Makes: 4 servings

- 1 **pound cooked turkey, chopped**
- 1 **16-ounce jar chunky salsa**
- 1 **15-ounce can cannellini (white kidney) beans, rinsed and drained**
- ⅔ **cup water**
- 1 **teaspoon chili powder**
- 1 **egg, beaten**
- 1 **8.5-ounce package corn bread mix**
- ¼ **cup water**
- ¼ **cup shredded cheddar cheese (optional)**
- **Slivered scallions (optional)**
- **Chili powder (optional)**

1 In a Dutch oven, combine turkey, salsa, beans, the ⅔ cup water, and the 1 teaspoon chili powder. Bring to boiling.

2 Meanwhile, in a medium bowl, stir together egg, corn bread mix, and the ¼ cup water just until moistened. Drop by large spoonfuls on top of boiling turkey mixture.

3 Reduce heat. Cover and simmer for 10 to 15 minutes or until a wooden pick inserted into a dumpling comes out clean. If desired, top with cheese, scallions, and additional chili powder.

Nutrition facts per serving: 555 cal., 15 g total fat (4 g sat. fat), 140 mg chol., 1618 mg sodium, 64 g carb., 11 g dietary fiber, 47 g protein.

zesty BLACK BEAN CHILI

Prep: 10 minutes
Cook: 20 minutes
Makes: 4 servings

1 16-ounce jar chunky salsa

1 15- to 16-ounce can black beans, rinsed and drained

1½ cups vegetable juice or hot-style vegetable juice

8 ounces fully cooked turkey kielbasa (Polish sausage), halved lengthwise and sliced

¼ cup water

2 teaspoons chili powder

2 cloves garlic, minced, or ¼ teaspoon garlic powder

Sour cream, sliced scallion, and/or peeled and chopped avocado (optional)

1 In a large saucepan, stir together salsa, beans, vegetable juice, turkey kielbasa, water, chili powder, and garlic. Bring to boiling; reduce heat. Simmer, covered, for 20 minutes, stirring occasionally.

2 Ladle chili into bowls. If desired, top with sour cream, scallion, and/or avocado.

Nutrition facts per serving: 210 cal., 5 g total fat (2 g sat. fat), 35 mg chol., 1878 mg sodium, 28 g carb., 6 g dietary fiber, 16 g protein.

all-american CHILI

Prep: 10 minutes
Cook: 6 hours (low) or
4 hours (high)
Makes: 6 servings

1½ **pounds lean ground beef**

2 **onions, chopped**

1 **yellow sweet pepper,**
seeded and chopped

2 **garlic cloves, minced**

2 **15.5-ounce cans kidney**
beans, rinsed and
drained

1 **14.5-ounce can diced**
tomatoes, drained

1 **8-ounce can no-salt-**
added tomato sauce

1 **cup reduced-sodium**
chicken broth

3 **tablespoons chili powder**

1 **teaspoon ground cumin**

1 **teaspoon dried oregano**

½ **teaspoon salt**

1 **8.5-ounce box corn bread**
mix, prepared according
to package directions
(optional)

1 Combine beef, onions, pepper, garlic, beans, tomatoes, tomato sauce, broth, 2 tablespoons of the chili powder, and ½ teaspoon each of the cumin and the oregano in slow cooker. Cover and cook on low-heat setting for 6 hours or on high-heat setting for 4 hours.

2 Remove cover and stir in remaining 1 tablespoon chili powder, ½ teaspoon each cumin and oregano, and salt. Serve with corn bread, if desired.

Nutrition facts per serving: 353 cal., 7 g total fat (3 g sat. fat), 71 mg chol., 710 mg sodium, 37 g carb., 13 g dietary fiber, 35 g protein.

barbecue CHILI

Three kinds of beans add a variety of color and texture to this sure-to-please chili.

Prep: 25 minutes
Cook: 8 to 10 hours (low)
or 4 to 5 hours
(high)
Makes: 10 to 12 servings

1 pound ground beef

1 cup chopped onion

2 cloves garlic, finely
   chopped

1 14.5-ounce can stewed
   tomatoes, cut up

1 cup ketchup

⅓ cup packed brown sugar

¼ cup chili powder

¼ cup molasses

¼ cup Worcestershire sauce

1 tablespoon ground cumin

1 tablespoon dry mustard

2 15- to 16-ounce cans dark
   red kidney beans,
   drained and rinsed

2 15- to 16-ounce cans
   pinto beans, drained
   and rinsed

1 15-ounce can white
   cannellini beans, drained
   and rinsed

10 to 12 cooked bacon strips
   (optional)

   Fresh jalapeño chile
   rings* (optional)

① In a large skillet, cook ground beef, onion, and garlic over medium-high heat until beef is cooked through, stirring to break into bite-size pieces. Drain off fat. Transfer to 5- to 6-quart slow cooker.

② Add tomatoes with their juices, ketchup, brown sugar, chili powder, molasses, Worcestershire sauce, cumin, and mustard to mixture in slow cooker; stir to combine. Stir in kidney, pinto, and cannellini beans. Cover and cook on low-heat setting for 8 to 10 hours or on high-heat setting for 4 to 5 hours.

③ To serve, ladle chili into bowls. If desired, top each serving with a strip of bacon and jalapeño rings.

Nutrition facts per serving: 381 cal., 6 g total fat (2 g sat. fat), 24 mg chol., 1172 mg sodium, 62 g carb., 13 g dietary fiber, 23 g protein.

*Tip: Because chile peppers contain volatile oils that can burn your skin and eyes, avoid direct contact with them as much as possible. When working with chile peppers, wear plastic or rubber gloves. If your bare hands do touch the peppers, wash your hands and nails well with soap and warm water.

cincinnati CHILI

Prep: 30 minutes
Cook: 8 to 10 hours (low) or 4 to 5 hours (high)
Makes: 6 servings

- 1 **bay leaf**
- ½ **teaspoon whole allspice**
- ½ **teaspoon whole cloves**
- 2 **pounds lean ground beef**
- 2 **cups chopped onions (2 large)**
- 1 **15-ounce can dark red kidney beans, rinsed and drained**
- 1 **15-ounce can tomato sauce**
- 1½ **cups water**
- 3 **tablespoons chili powder**
- 4 **cloves garlic, minced**
- 1 **teaspoon Worcestershire sauce**
- ¾ **teaspoon ground cumin**
- ¾ **teaspoon ground cinnamon**
- ½ **teaspoon salt**
- ¼ **teaspoon cayenne pepper**
- ½ **ounce unsweetened chocolate, chopped**
- 12 **ounces dried spaghetti, cooked and well drained**
- 1 **cup shredded cheddar cheese (4 ounces)**

1 For a spice bag, cut a 4-inch square from a double thickness of 100% cotton cheesecloth. Place bay leaf, allspice, and cloves in the center of the cheesecloth square. Bring up corners of the cheesecloth; tie closed with clean kitchen string.

2 In a large skillet, cook meat over medium heat until brown. Drain off fat. In a 3½- or 4-quart slow cooker, combine meat, onion, beans, tomato sauce, the water, chili powder, garlic, Worcestershire sauce, cumin, cinnamon, salt, and cayenne. Stir in spice bag.

3 Cover and cook on low-heat setting for 8 to 10 hours or on high-heat setting for 4 to 5 hours. Stir in chocolate for the last 30 minutes of cooking. Remove and discard spice bag.

4 To serve, ladle chili over spaghetti. Sprinkle each serving with cheese.

Nutrition facts per serving: 743 cal., 32 g total fat (14 g sat. fat), 123 mg chol., 953 mg sodium, 69 g carb., 10 g dietary fiber, 48 g protein.

fruit AND NUT CHILI

Chocolate and spicy ingredients are a common pairing in chili creations. With the addition of curry, almonds, and apples, this tantalizing version is a recipe you must try.

Prep: 25 minutes
Cook: 8 to 10 hours (low)
　　　or 4 to 5 hours
　　　(high)
Makes: 8 servings

1½ **pounds lean ground beef**

2 **large onions, chopped (2 cups)**

3 **cloves garlic, minced**

2 **14.5-ounce cans diced tomatoes, undrained**

1 **15-ounce can red kidney beans, rinsed and drained**

1 **15-ounce can tomato sauce**

1 **14-ounce can chicken broth**

2¼ **cups chopped green, red, and/or yellow sweet peppers**

2 **medium cooking apples,* cored and chopped (1⅓ cups)**

2 **4-ounce cans diced green chile peppers, drained**

3 **tablespoons chili powder**

2 **tablespoons unsweetened cocoa powder**

1 **tablespoon curry powder**

1 **teaspoon ground cinnamon**

⅔ **cup slivered almonds**

Shredded cheddar cheese, raisins, and/or plain yogurt (optional)

1　In a 12-inch skillet, cook ground beef, onion, and garlic until meat is brown and onion is tender. Drain off fat. Transfer meat mixture to a 6-quart slow cooker.

2　Add tomatoes, beans, tomato sauce, and broth. Stir in sweet pepper, apples, chile peppers, chili powder, cocoa powder, curry powder, and cinnamon.

3　Cover and cook on low-heat setting for 8 to 10 hours or on high-heat setting for 4 to 5 hours.

4　Top individual servings with almonds and, if desired, cheese, raisins, and/or yogurt.

Nutrition facts per serving: 357 cal., 16 g total fat (4 g sat. fat), 54 mg chol., 782 mg sodium, 34 g carb., 10 g dietary fiber, 26 g protein.

*Tip: Use Granny Smith or Jonathan apples for the best results.

beef AND RED BEAN CHILI

If you usually make chili with hamburger, give this recipe a go for something different. You'll love the way chunky pieces of succulent pot roast add a robust, meaty aspect to the stew.

Prep: 25 minutes
Stand: 1 hour
Cook: 10 to 12 hours (low) or 5 to 6 hours (high)
Makes: 8 servings

- 1 cup dried red beans or kidney beans
- 2 pounds boneless beef chuck pot roast, trimmed and cut into 1-inch pieces
- 1 cup coarsely chopped onion
- 1 tablespoon olive oil
- 1 15-ounce can tomato sauce
- 1 14.5-ounce can diced tomatoes with mild green chile peppers
- 1 can (14 ounces) beef broth
- 1 or 2 chipotle chiles in adobo sauce, finely chopped,* plus 2 teaspoons adobo sauce
- 2 teaspoons dried oregano
- 1 teaspoon ground cumin
- ¾ cup chopped red sweet pepper
- ¼ cup chopped fresh cilantro

1 Rinse beans. Place beans in large saucepan or Dutch oven. Add enough water to cover by 2 inches. Bring to a boil; reduce heat. Simmer, uncovered, for 10 minutes. Remove from heat. Cover; let stand for 1 hour.

2 Meanwhile, in a large skillet cook half of the pot roast pieces and the onion in hot oil over medium-high heat until beef is brown. Using a slotted spoon, transfer to 3½- or 4-quart slow cooker. Repeat with remaining pot roast pieces. Add tomato sauce, undrained tomatoes, beef broth, chipotle chiles and adobo sauce, oregano, and cumin to mixture in cooker; stir to combine. Drain and rinse beans; stir into mixture in slow cooker.

3 Cover and cook on low-heat setting for 10 to 12 hours or on high-heat setting for 5 to 6 hours. Top each serving with sweet pepper and cilantro.

Nutrition facts per serving: 269 cal., 6 g total fat (2 g sat. fat), 67 mg chol., 550 mg sodium, 21 g carb., 8 g dietary fiber, 32 g protein.

*Tip: Because chiles contain volatile oils that can burn your skin and eyes, avoid direct contact with them as much as possible. When working with chiles, wear plastic or rubber gloves. If your bare hands do touch the peppers, wash your hands and nails well with soap and warm water.

chili CON CARNE

Prep: 21 minutes
Slow Cook: 6 hours (low)
or 4 hours
(high)
Makes: 6 servings

1 tablespoon plus
1 teaspoon olive oil

2 pounds boneless beef
round steak, trimmed
and cut into ½-inch
cubes

3 cloves garlic, minced

1 large onion, finely
chopped

3 tablespoons plus
1 teaspoon chili powder

3½ teaspoons ground cumin

1 teaspoon salt

½ teaspoon cayenne pepper

1 package (10 ounces)
frozen corn

3¾ cups water

3 tablespoons finely ground
cornmeal

3 tablespoons water

Sour cream, sliced
avocado, and cilantro
(optional)

1 Heat 1 tablespoon of the oil in a large nonstick skillet over medium-high heat. Add beef to skillet and cook, stirring occasionally, for 8 minutes, draining any accumulated fat. Transfer beef to slow cooker; reduce heat to medium. Add remaining 1 teaspoon oil to skillet; add garlic and onion and cook, stirring, for 2 minutes. Stir in 3 tablespoons chili powder, 2 teaspoons cumin, ½ teaspoon salt, and ¼ teaspoon cayenne; cook for 1 minute, stirring constantly.

2 Scrape skillet contents into slow cooker and add corn and 3¾ cups water (enough to cover by 1 inch). Cover and cook on low-heat setting for 6 hours or on high-heat setting for 4 hours.

3 When there is 1 hour cook time remaining, stir together cornmeal and 3 tablespoons water. Stir in cornmeal paste, remaining 1 teaspoon chili powder, 1½ teaspoons cumin, ½ teaspoon salt, and ¼ teaspoon cayenne; cook for 1 more hour or until thickened. Garnish with sour cream, avocado, and cilantro, if desired.

Nutrition facts per serving: 374 cal., 17 g total fat (5 g sat. fat), 60 mg chol., 536 mg sodium, 21 g carb., 4 g dietary fiber, 36 g protein.

chipotle STEAK CHILI

Prep: 30 minutes
Cook: 1 hour
Makes: 8 servings

1½ **pounds boneless beef shoulder top blade steak (flat iron)**

1 **tablespoon vegetable oil**

2 **cups chopped onions (2 large)**

1 **cup chopped green sweet peppers (2 small)**

4 **cloves garlic, minced**

2 **15- to 16-ounce cans kidney beans, pinto beans, and/or black beans, rinsed and drained**

2 **14.5-ounce can diced tomatoes, undrained**

1 **15-ounce can tomato sauce**

½ **cup water**

2 **tablespoons chili powder**

1 **to 2 teaspoons chopped canned chipotle chile peppers in adobo sauce***

1 **teaspoon dried basil, crushed**

½ **teaspoon ground black pepper**

Shredded cheddar cheese (optional)

Sour cream (optional)

1️⃣ Trim fat from meat. Cut meat into ¾-inch pieces. In a 4-quart Dutch oven, heat oil over medium heat. Brown meat, half at a time, in hot oil. Remove meat, reserving drippings in Dutch oven. Cook onions, sweet peppers, and garlic in drippings until tender.

2️⃣ Return meat to Dutch oven. Stir beans, tomatoes, tomato sauce, the water, chili powder, chile peppers, basil, and black pepper into meat mixture. Bring to boiling; reduce heat. Cover and simmer for about 1 hour or until meat is tender, stirring occasionally. If desired, top each serving with cheese and/or sour cream.

Nutrition facts per serving: 288 cal., 8 g total fat (3 g sat. fat), 54 mg chol., 639 mg sodium, 32 g carb., 8 g dietary fiber, 24 g protein.

*Tip: Because chile peppers contain volatile oils that can burn your skin and eyes, avoid direct contact with them as much as possible. When working with chile peppers, wear plastic or rubber gloves. If your bare hands do touch the peppers, wash your hands and nails well with soap and warm water.

white CHILI WITH SAUSAGE

Prep: 15 minutes
Cook: 20 minutes
Makes: 6 servings

1½ **pounds bulk pork sausage**

1 **cup chopped onion (1 large)**

4 **cloves garlic, minced**

2 **19-ounce cans cannellini beans, rinsed and drained**

2 **14-ounce cans reduced-sodium chicken broth**

1 **14.5-ounce can white or yellow whole kernel corn, drained**

1 **fresh poblano chile pepper, seeded and finely chopped***

⅓ **cup lime juice**

¼ **teaspoon ground white pepper**

Crushed white corn tortilla chips

In a 4-quart Dutch oven, cook and stir sausage, onion, and garlic over medium heat until sausage is no longer pink. Stir in beans, broth, corn, chile pepper, lime juice, and white pepper. Bring to boiling; reduce heat. Simmer, covered, for 20 minutes. Serve with crushed chips.

Nutrition facts per serving: 660 cal., 37 g total fat (14 g sat. fat), 65 mg chol., 1464 mg sodium, 54 g carb., 10 g dietary fiber, 28 g protein.

*Tip: Because chile peppers contain volatile oils that can burn your skin and eyes, avoid direct contact with them as much as possible. When working with chile peppers, wear plastic or rubber gloves. If your bare hands do touch the peppers, wash your hands and nails well with soap and warm water.

hearty PORK CHILI

Serve this pork-filled chili at an after-the-game open house or for a bowl-watching party. Set out an assortment of toppers so guests can personalize their bowls of chili.

Prep: 25 minutes
Cook: 8 to 10 hours (low)
or 4 to 5 hours
(high)
Makes: 8 servings

1½ **pounds boneless pork shoulder roast, trimmed and cut into 1-inch cubes**

2 **15-ounce cans black beans, kidney beans, and/or chickpeas, rinsed and drained**

2 **14.5-ounce cans diced tomatoes with onions and garlic**

1 **10-ounce can chopped tomatoes with green chile peppers**

1½ **cups chopped celery**

1 **cup chopped green sweet pepper**

3 **cloves garlic, chopped**

1 **tablespoon chili powder**

1 **teaspoon ground cumin**

1 **teaspoon dried oregano**

2 **cups vegetable juice or tomato juice**

Toppers (such as shredded Mexican-blend cheese, sour cream, sliced scallions, chopped fresh cilantro, and/or sliced jalapeño chile peppers* (optional)

1 In 5- to 6-quart slow cooker, combine pork, beans or chickpeas, tomatoes with their juices, celery, sweet pepper, garlic, chili powder, cumin, and oregano. Stir in vegetable juice.

2 Cover and cook on low-heat setting for 8 to 10 hours or on high-heat setting for 4 to 5 hours. If desired, serve with toppers.

Nutrition facts per serving: 251 cal., 6 g total fat (2 g sat. fat), 55 mg chol., 1126 mg sodium, 28 g carb., 8 g dietary fiber, 27 g protein.

*Tip: Because chiles contain volatile oils that can burn your skin and eyes, avoid direct contact with them as much as possible. When working with chiles, wear plastic or rubber gloves. If your bare hands do touch the peppers, wash your hands and nails well with soap and warm water.

chunky BEER-PORK CHILI

Start to Finish: 30 minutes
Makes: 4 servings

12 ounces pork tenderloin

2 teaspoons chili powder

2 teaspoons ground cumin

1 small onion, chopped

2 teaspoons bottled minced garlic

1 tablespoon cooking oil

1 yellow or red sweet pepper, cut into ½-inch pieces

1 cup beer or beef broth

½ cup bottled picante sauce or salsa

1 to 2 tablespoons finely chopped canned chipotle chile pepper in adobo sauce*

1 15- to 16-ounce can small red beans or pinto beans, rinsed and drained

½ cup sour cream

Fresh cilantro or flat-leaf parsley sprigs (optional)

1 Trim fat from meat. Cut meat into ¾-inch pieces; transfer to medium bowl. Add chili powder and cumin; toss gently to coat.

2 In a large saucepan, cook onion and garlic in hot oil over medium-high heat for about 3 minutes or until tender. Add meat. Cook and stir until meat is brown.

3 Stir in sweet pepper, beer, picante sauce, and chipotle chile pepper. Bring to boiling; reduce heat. Cover and simmer for about 5 minutes or until pork is tender. Stir in beans; heat through.

4 Top each serving with sour cream. If desired, garnish with cilantro.

Nutrition facts per serving: 328 cal., 11 g total fat (4 g sat. fat), 65 mg chol., 625 mg sodium, 29 g carb., 7 g dietary fiber, 26 g protein.

*Tip: Because chile peppers contain volatile oils that can burn your skin and eyes, avoid direct contact with them as much as possible. When working with chile peppers, wear plastic or rubber gloves. If your bare hands do touch the peppers, wash your hands and nails well with soap and warm water.

pineapple-pork CHILI

This Hawaiian-inspired chili features pork, kidney beans, and a surprise ingredient—pineapple salsa.

Start to Finish: 20 minutes
Makes: 4 servings

1 **pound ground pork or beef**

1 **16-ounce jar pineapple salsa***

1 **15-ounce can red kidney beans, rinsed and drained**

1 **8-ounce can tomato sauce**

1 **tablespoon chili powder**

   Pineapple slices (optional)

In a 3-quart saucepan, cook meat over medium heat until brown. Drain off fat. Stir in salsa, beans, tomato sauce, and chili powder. Bring to boiling; reduce heat. Simmer, uncovered, for 10 minutes. If desired, garnish with pineapple slices.

Nutrition facts per serving: 329 cal., 9 g total fat (4 g sat. fat), 53 mg chol., 852 mg sodium, 44 g carb., 11 g dietary fiber, 22 g protein.

*Tip:** If you can't find pineapple salsa, use regular salsa and add ⅓ to ½ cup crushed pineapple.

portobello CHILI

Prep: 15 minutes
Cook: 6 to 8 hours (low)
or 3 to 4 hours
(high)
Makes: 4 servings

2 **15-ounce cans red kidney beans, rinsed and drained**

2 **14.5-ounce cans diced tomatoes with basil and oregano**

6 **cups coarsely chopped fresh portobello mushrooms (1 pound)**

1 **cup chopped onion (1 large)**

1 **tablespoon chili powder**

2 **teaspoons ground cumin**

2 **cloves garlic, minced**

Sour cream (optional)

1 In a 3½- or 4-quart slow cooker, combine beans, undrained tomatoes, mushrooms, onion, chili powder, cumin, and garlic.

2 Cover and cook on low-heat setting for 6 to 8 hours or on high-heat setting for 3 to 4 hours. If desired, top each serving with sour cream.

Nutrition facts per serving: 322 cal., 2 g total fat (0 g sat. fat), 0 mg chol., 1816 mg sodium, 63 g carb., 18 g dietary fiber, 18 g protein.

white BEAN AND SWEET POTATO CHILI

Start to Finish: 30 minutes
Makes: 6 servings

1 large onion, chopped (1 cup)

3 cloves garlic, minced

1 tablespoon cooking oil

2 15- to 19-ounce cans cannellini beans (white kidney beans), rinsed and drained

2 14.5-ounce cans Mexican-style stewed tomatoes, cut up, undrained

1 14-ounce can chicken broth

1 4-ounce can diced green chile peppers

1 15-ounce can cut sweet potatoes, drained and cut into bite-size pieces

In a 4-quart Dutch oven, cook onion and garlic in hot oil over medium heat until tender. Stir in beans, tomatoes, broth, and green chiles. Bring to boiling, reduce heat. Stir in sweet potatoes. Simmer, uncovered, for 15 minutes.

Nutrition facts per serving: 162 cal., 3 g total fat (0 g sat. fat), 1 mg chol., 1007 mg sodium, 33 g carb., 7 g dietary fiber, 10 g protein.

three-bean VEGETARIAN CHILI

Prep: 20 minutes
Cook: 6 to 8 hours (low)
or 3 to 4 hours
(high)
Makes: 4 servings

1 15-ounce can no-salt-
added red kidney beans,
rinsed and drained

1 15-ounce can small white
beans, rinsed and
drained

1 15-ounce can low-sodium
black beans, rinsed and
drained

1 14.5-ounce can diced
tomatoes with green
chile peppers, undrained

1 cup beer or chicken broth

3 tablespoons chocolate-
flavored syrup

1 tablespoon chili powder

2 teaspoons Cajun
seasoning

Sour cream (optional)

Shredded cheddar cheese
(optional)

1 In a 3½- or 4-quart slow cooker, combine kidney beans, white beans, black beans, tomatoes, beer, chocolate syrup, chili powder, and Cajun seasoning.

2 Cover and cook on low-heat setting for 6 to 8 hours or on high-heat setting for 3 to 4 hours. If desired, top individual servings with sour cream and cheese.

Nutrition facts per serving: 308 cal., 1 g total fat (0 g sat. fat), 0 mg chol., 569 mg sodium, 60 g carb., 21 g dietary fiber, 21 g protein.

white bean AND CUMIN CHILI

Toasting the cumin seeds brings out a deep, nutty flavor. You'll know the cumin is ready when your kitchen is consumed with its fragrant aroma.

Prep: 25 minutes
Cook: 8 to 9 hours (low)
     or 4 to 4½ hours
     (high)
Makes: 6 servings

- 2 19-ounce cans cannellini beans (white kidney beans), rinsed and drained
- 2 14.5-ounce cans no-salt-added diced tomatoes
- 1½ cups peeled, seeded, and coarsely chopped butternut squash (about 12 ounces)
- 1½ cups chopped onions
- 1 12-ounce can light beer
- 1 chipotle chile pepper in adobo sauce, finely chopped*
- 1 tablespoon cumin seeds, toasted and ground**
- 3 cloves garlic, minced
- ½ teaspoon salt
- ⅓ cup light sour cream
- 2 tablespoons lime juice
- 1 tablespoon snipped fresh chives
  Small lime wedges (optional)

1 Combine beans, undrained tomatoes, squash, onions, beer, chile pepper, cumin, garlic, and salt in a 3½- or 4-quart slow cooker.

2 Cover and cook on low-heat setting for 8 to 9 hours or on high-heat setting for 4 to 4½ hours.

3 Combine sour cream, lime juice, and snipped chives in a small bowl. Spoon chili into bowls; top with sour cream mixture. Garnish with lime wedges, if desired.

Nutrition facts per serving: 140 cal., 1 g total fat (1 g sat. fat), 4 mg chol., 406 mg sodium, 28 g carb., 7 g dietary fiber, 7 g protein.

*Tip: Because chile peppers contain volatile oils that can burn your skin and eyes, avoid direct contact with them as much as possible. When working with chile peppers, wear plastic or rubber gloves. If your bare hands do touch the peppers, wash your hands and nails well with soap and warm water.

**Tip: To toast and grind cumin seeds, place cumin in a dry skillet over medium heat. Cook for 2 to 3 minutes or until cumin becomes fragrant, shaking skillet occasionally. (Avoid overcooking cumin seeds, which can make them bitter.) Remove from heat; allow to cool before crushing with a mortar and pestle or food processor.

veggie chili WITH CHEESE TOPPING

A cheddar and cream cheese topping provides a soothing counterpoint to this spunky cocoa-accented chili.

Prep: 20 minutes
Cook: 45 minutes
Makes: 6 servings

1¼ **cups finely chopped zucchini**

¾ **cup finely chopped carrot**

1 **scallion, chopped**

1 **teaspoon bottled minced garlic**

2 **15-ounce cans hot-style chili beans in chili sauce**

2 **14.5-ounce cans diced tomatoes**

¼ **cup ketchup**

1 **tablespoon unsweetened cocoa powder**

1 **teaspoon chili powder**

1 **teaspoon ground cumin**

1 **teaspoon bottled hot pepper sauce**

¼ **teaspoon dried oregano, crushed**

½ **of an 8-ounce tub cream cheese with chive and onion**

2 **tablespoons milk**

½ **cup shredded cheddar cheese (2 ounces)**

Scallion strips (optional)

1 Coat a large saucepan with cooking spray; heat over medium heat. Add zucchini, carrot, chopped scallion, and garlic; cook for 2 minutes. Add undrained chili beans, undrained tomatoes, ketchup, cocoa powder, chili powder, cumin, hot pepper sauce, and oregano. Bring to boiling; reduce heat. Simmer, uncovered, for about 45 minutes or until desired consistency, stirring occasionally. Season to taste with salt and black pepper.

2 Meanwhile, in a small bowl stir together cream cheese and milk until smooth. Stir in cheddar cheese. To serve, ladle chili into bowls. Spoon some of the cream cheese mixture onto each serving. If desired, garnish with scallion strips.

Nutrition facts per serving: 281 cal., 13 g total fat (5 g sat. fat), 30 mg chol., 1183 mg sodium, 39 g carb., 5 g dietary fiber, 13 g protein.

vegetarian CHILI WITH POLENTA

Prep: 20 minutes
Cook: 20 minutes
Makes: 4 servings

1 tablespoon olive oil

½ cup chopped onion (1 medium)

1 cup loose-pack frozen hash brown potatoes

1 cup chopped zucchini

1 10-ounce can diced tomatoes with green chile peppers, undrained

1 8-ounce can tomato sauce

2 teaspoons chili powder

2 cloves garlic, minced

1 15- to 16-ounce can kidney beans, rinsed and drained

1 16-ounce tube refrigerated polenta, cut into 8 slices

½ cup shredded Monterey Jack cheese (2 ounces)

Sour cream (optional)

1 In a large skillet, heat oil over medium heat. Add onion; cook and stir until tender. Stir in potatoes, zucchini, tomatoes, tomato sauce, chili powder, and garlic. Bring to boiling; reduce heat. Cover and simmer for 15 minutes. Stir in beans. Simmer, uncovered, for 5 minutes more or until desired consistency.

2 Meanwhile, prepare polenta according to package directions. Serve with chili. Sprinkle with Monterey Jack cheese. If desired, top each serving with sour cream.

Nutrition facts per serving: 350 cal., 9 g total fat (3 g sat. fat), 15 mg chol., 1251 mg sodium, 58 g carb., 12 g dietary fiber, 17 g protein.

sides

Tomato-Pesto Scones with Kalamata Olives, *page 200*

tomato-pesto SCONES WITH KALAMATA OLIVES

Prep: 25 minutes
Bake: 12 minutes
Oven: 425°F
Makes: 9 to 15 servings

1 cup dried tomatoes (3-ounces; not oil-packed)

2 cups all-purpose flour

1 0.5-ounce envelope dry pesto sauce mix

2 teaspoons baking powder

½ teaspoon baking soda

¼ cup butter

¾ cup milk

1 egg yolk

½ cup pitted kalamata olives, coarsely chopped and drained

1 tablespoon snipped fresh rosemary

Fresh rosemary sprigs

1 tablespoon olive oil

1 In a small bowl, pour enough boiling water over dried tomatoes to cover. Let stand for 10 minutes; drain well. Remove 2 of the dried tomatoes; set aside. Chop remaining tomatoes and set aside.

2 Meanwhile, preheat oven to 425°F. Line a large baking sheet with parchment paper; set aside. In a large bowl, combine flour, pesto sauce mix, baking powder, and baking soda. Using a pastry blender, cut in butter until mixture resembles coarse crumbs. Make a well in center of the flour mixture.

3 In a medium bowl, combine milk and egg yolk. Add milk mixture all at once to flour mixture. Add the chopped tomatoes, olives, and snipped rosemary. Using a fork, stir just until moistened.

4 Turn dough out onto a lightly floured surface. Knead dough by folding and gently pressing it for 10 to 12 strokes or just until dough holds together. With floured hands, pat or lightly roll dough to a 9x6-inch rectangle on prepared baking sheet. Using a sharp knife, cut scones into 9 to 15 diamond pieces (do not separate). Lightly press the 2 reserved tomatoes and a few rosemary sprigs into top of dough. Brush with olive oil. Bake for 12 to 14 minutes or until light brown. Gently pull or cut scones to separate. Serve warm.

Nutrition facts per serving: 208 cal., 9 g total fat (4 g sat. fat), 39 mg chol., 595 mg sodium, 27 g carb., 2 g dietary fiber, 5 g protein.

checkerboard ROLLS

Prep: 15 minutes
Chill: 8 to 24 hours
Stand: 45 minutes
Bake: 20 minutes
Oven: 375°F
Makes: 16 servings

- 2 **tablespoons poppy seeds**
- 2 **tablespoons sesame seeds**
- 1 **teaspoon lemon-pepper seasoning**
- 2 **tablespoons yellow cornmeal**
- 2 **tablespoons grated or finely shredded Parmesan cheese**
- 3 **tablespoons butter, melted**
- 16 **1.3-ounce pieces frozen white roll dough**

1 Grease a 9x9x2-inch baking pan. In a shallow dish, combine poppy seeds, sesame seeds, and lemon-pepper seasoning. In another shallow dish, combine cornmeal and cheese. Place butter in a third shallow dish.

2 Working quickly, roll frozen dough pieces in butter, then in one of the seasoning mixtures to lightly coat. (Coat half of the rolls with one seasoning mixture and the remaining rolls with the other seasoning mixture.) Alternate rolls in the prepared baking pan. Cover with greased plastic wrap. Let thaw in the refrigerator for 8 to 24 hours.

3 Remove pan from refrigerator; uncover and let stand at room temperature for 45 minutes. Meanwhile, preheat oven to 375°F.

4 Bake rolls for 20 to 25 minutes or until golden. Remove rolls from pan; cool slightly on a wire rack.

Nutrition facts per serving: 136 cal., 5 g total fat (2 g sat. fat), 6 mg chol., 189 mg sodium, 19 g carb., 1 g dietary fiber, 4 g protein.

Garlic-Herb Checkerboard Rolls: Prepare as directed, except substitute 1 teaspoon dried Italian seasoning, crushed, and ½ teaspoon garlic powder for the lemon-pepper seasoning.

quick SEED BREAD

Prep: 20 minutes
Bake: 45 minutes
Stand: Overnight
Oven: 350°F
Makes: 1 loaf (14 servings)

1½ **cups all-purpose flour**

½ **cup whole wheat flour**

¾ **cup packed brown sugar**

½ **cup dry-roasted sunflower kernels**

⅓ **cup flaxseed meal**

2 **tablespoons sesame seeds**

2 **tablespoons poppy seeds**

1 **teaspoon baking powder**

½ **teaspoon baking soda**

½ **teaspoon salt**

1 **egg**

1¼ **cups buttermilk or sour milk***

¼ **cup vegetable oil**

4 **teaspoons sesame seeds, poppy seeds and/or dry-roasted sunflower kernels**

① Preheat oven to 350°F. Grease the bottom and ½ inch up the sides of a 9x5x3-inch loaf pan; set aside.

② In a large bowl, stir together the flours, brown sugar, ½ cup sunflower kernels, ground flaxseed, the 2 tablespoons sesame seeds, the 2 tablespoons poppy seeds, the baking powder, baking soda, and salt. Make a well in the center of the flour mixture. In a medium bowl, beat egg with a fork; stir in buttermilk and oil. Add egg mixture all at once to flour mixture. Stir just until moistened (batter should be lumpy). Spread batter into prepared pan. Sprinkle with the 4 teaspoons seeds.

③ Bake for 45 to 55 minutes or until a wooden toothpick inserted near the center comes out clean. Cool in pan on a wire rack for 10 minutes. Remove from pan. Cool completely on wire rack. Wrap and store bread overnight before slicing.

Nutrition facts per serving: 216 cal., 10 g total fat (1 g sat. fat), 16 mg chol., 180 mg sodium, 28 g carb., 2 g dietary fiber, 5 g protein.

*Tip: To make 1¼ cups sour milk, place 4 teaspoons lemon juice or vinegar in a glass measuring cup. Add enough milk to make 1¼ cups total liquid; stir. Let stand for 5 minutes before using.

pull-apart CORNMEAL DINNER ROLLS

Prep: 30 minutes
Rise: 1½ hours
Bake: 12 minutes
Oven: 400°F
Makes: 32 rolls

1	**cup milk**
¼	**cup sugar**
¼	**cup butter, cut up**
¼	**cup yellow cornmeal**
1	**teaspoon salt**
1	**package active dry yeast**
¼	**cup warm water (105°F to 115°F)**
1	**egg, lightly beaten**
3¾	**to 4¼ cups all-purpose flour**
2	**tablespoons butter, melted**
1	**to 2 tablespoons yellow cornmeal**

1 In a small saucepan, heat and stir milk, sugar, the ¼ cup butter, the ¼ cup cornmeal, and the salt just until warm (105°F to 115°F) and butter almost melts. In a large bowl, dissolve yeast in the warm water. Add egg and warm milk mixture. Using a wooden spoon, stir in enough flour to make a soft dough.

2 Turn dough out onto a lightly floured surface. Knead in enough of the remaining flour to make a moderately soft dough that is smooth and elastic (about 3 minutes total). Shape dough into a ball. Place in a lightly greased bowl; turn once to grease surface of dough. Cover; let rise in a warm place until double in size (about 1 hour).

3 Punch dough down. Turn dough out onto a lightly floured surface. Cover and let rest for 10 minutes. Meanwhile, grease a 15x10x1-inch baking pan.

4 Roll or pat dough into a 10x8-inch rectangle. Cut into 2½x1-inch strips. Arrange strips in prepared pan, leaving about ¼ inch between each strip. Cover; let rise in a warm place until nearly double in size (about 30 minutes).

5 Preheat oven to 400°F. Brush rolls with the melted butter. Sprinkle with the 1 to 2 tablespoons cornmeal. Bake for 12 to 15 minutes or until tops are golden brown. Cool slightly. Remove from pan and serve warm.

Nutrition facts per roll: 90 cal., 3 g total fat (2 g sat. fat), 13 mg chol., 94 mg sodium, 14 g carb., 1 g dietary fiber, 2 g protein.

cheddar AND BACON LOAF

Prep: 10 minutes
Bake: 10 minutes
Oven: 350°F
Makes: 12 servings

1 **1-pound loaf baguette-style French bread**

½ **of an 8-ounce package shredded sharp cheddar cheese (1 cup)**

½ **cup butter, softened**

⅓ **cup cooked bacon pieces**

2 **medium scallions, sliced (¼ cup)**

2 **teaspoons yellow mustard**

1 **teaspoon lemon juice**

1 Preheat oven to 350°F. Use a serrated knife to cut bread crosswise into 1-inch slices, cutting to but not through the bottom crust.

2 In a small bowl, stir together cheese, butter, bacon, scallions, mustard, and lemon juice. Spread mixture between slices of bread. Wrap loaf in foil.

3 Bake for 10 to 15 minutes or until bread is heated through and cheese is melted.

Nutrition facts per serving: 238 cal., 13 g total fat (8 g sat. fat), 35 mg chol., 461 mg sodium, 22 g carb., 1 g dietary fiber, 10 g protein.

corn BREAD

Prep: 10 minutes
Bake: 15 minutes
Oven: 400°F
Makes: 8 to 10 servings

 1 **cup all-purpose flour**
¾ **cup cornmeal**
 2 **to 3 tablespoons sugar**
2½ **teaspoons baking powder**
¾ **teaspoon salt**
 1 **tablespoon butter**
 2 **eggs**
 1 **cup milk**
¼ **cup cooking oil or melted butter**

1 Preheat oven to 400°F. In a medium bowl, stir together the flour, cornmeal, sugar, baking powder, and salt; set aside.

2 Add the 1 tablespoon butter to an 8x8x2-inch baking pan, a 9x1½-inch round baking pan, or a 10-inch cast-iron skillet. Place pan in the preheated oven for about 3 minutes or until butter melts. Remove pan from oven; swirl butter to coat bottom and sides of pan.

3 Meanwhile, in a small bowl beat eggs with a fork; stir in milk and oil. Add egg mixture to flour mixture all at once; stir just until moistened (batter should be lumpy). Pour batter into the hot pan. Bake for 15 to 20 minutes or until a wooden toothpick inserted near the center comes out clean. Serve warm.

Nutrition facts per wedge: 219 cal., 10 g total fat (3 g sat. fat), 60 mg chol., 390 mg sodium, 26 g carb., 1 g dietary fiber, 5 g protein.

Double Corn Bread: Prepare as above, except fold ½ cup frozen whole kernel corn, thawed, into the batter.

Green Onion–Bacon Corn Bread: Prepare as above, except fold ⅓ cup cooked, crumbled bacon and ¼ cup sliced scallions into the batter.

Corn Muffins: Prepare as above, except omit the 1 tablespoon butter. Spoon batter into 12 greased 2½-inch muffin cups, filling each two-thirds full. Bake for about 15 minutes or until light brown and a wooden toothpick inserted in the centers comes out clean. Makes 12 muffins.

vegetable FLATBREADS WITH GOAT CHEESE

Prep: 25 minutes
Broil: 6 minutes
Oven: Broil
Makes: 4 servings

- ⅓ cup olive oil
- 1 medium yellow summer squash, quartered lengthwise and sliced
- ½ small red onion, sliced
- 1 small green sweet pepper, chopped
- 1 small red sweet pepper, chopped
- 1 medium carrot, chopped
- ½ cup fresh broccoli florets
- 4 cloves garlic, minced
- 2 roma tomatoes, chopped
- 12 pimiento-stuffed green olives, halved, plus 1 tablespoon liquid from jar
- 4 6- to 7½-inch flatbreads
- 8 ounces goat cheese, crumbled
- Ground black pepper

① Preheat broiler. In a 12-inch skillet, heat 2 tablespoons of the oil over medium-high heat. Add squash, onion, sweet peppers, carrot, broccoli, and garlic. Cook and stir for 3 minutes. Add tomatoes, olives, and olive liquid. Cook, uncovered, for 2 minutes more or until tender.

② Place flatbreads on large baking sheets. Lightly brush both sides with some of the remaining olive oil. Broil half at a time, 4 inches from the heat, for 1 to 2 minutes on each side or until lightly browned and toasted.

③ Using slotted spoon, remove vegetable mixture from skillet and spoon on toasted flatbreads. Top with cheese. Sprinkle with ⅛ teaspoon black pepper. Broil 4 inches from heat for 2 minutes or until cheese softens. Drizzle with remaining olive oil. Sprinkle with sea salt and more black pepper.

Nutrition facts per serving: 611 cal., 40 g total fat (15 g sat. fat), 45 mg chol., 894 mg sodium, 45 g carb., 5 g dietary fiber, 20 g protein.

swiss cheese–almond
FLATBREAD

Prep: 40 minutes
Rise: 1 hour 20 minutes
Bake: 25 minutes
Cool: 1 hour
Oven: 375°F
Makes: 2 rounds
       (24 servings)

3 to 3½ cups all-purpose flour

1 package active dry yeast

1 teaspoon salt

1¼ cups warm water (120°F to 130°F)

2 tablespoons olive oil

½ cup white whole wheat flour or whole wheat flour

⅔ cup finely shredded Swiss cheese

⅓ cup sliced almonds

½ teaspoon coarse sea salt

½ teaspoon cracked black pepper

1 In a large bowl, stir together 1¼ cups of the all-purpose flour, the yeast, and the 1 teaspoon salt. Add the warm water and 1 tablespoon of the oil. Beat with an electric mixer on low to medium speed for 30 seconds, scraping side of bowl constantly. Beat on high speed for 3 minutes. Using a wooden spoon, stir in whole wheat flour and as much of the remaining all-purpose flour as you can.

2 Turn out dough onto a lightly floured surface. Knead in enough of the remaining all-purpose flour to make a stiff dough that is smooth and elastic (8 to 10 minutes total). Shape dough into a ball. Place in a lightly greased bowl, turning once to grease surface. Cover and let rise in a warm place until double in size (about 1 hour).

3 Lightly grease two baking sheets. Punch down dough. Turn out on a lightly floured surface. Divide dough in half. Shape each dough portion into a ball. Place on prepared baking sheets. Cover; let rest for 10 minutes. Flatten each ball into a circle about 9 inches in diameter. Using your fingers, make ½-inch-deep indentations every 2 inches in dough (dust your fingers with flour if necessary). Brush with the remaining 1 tablespoon oil. Sprinkle with Swiss cheese, almonds, coarse salt, and pepper. Cover; let rise in a warm place until nearly double in size (about 20 minutes).

4 Meanwhile, preheat oven to 375°F. Bake for 25 to 30 minutes or until golden brown. Remove bread from baking sheets. Cool on wire racks.

Nutrition facts per serving: 97 cal., 3 g total fat (1 g sat. fat), 3 mg chol., 138 mg sodium, 14 g carb., 1 g dietary fiber, 3 g protein.

grape AND ROSEMARY FOCACCIA

As this bread bakes, the grapes become lightly roasted, turning soft and juicy.

Prep: 20 minutes
Rise: 30 minutes
Bake: 20 minutes
Oven: 450°F
Makes: 12 servings

- 1 **pound refrigerated or thawed frozen pizza dough**
- 2 **tablespoons extra-virgin olive oil**
- ½ **teaspoon coarse salt (kosher or sea salt)**
- ½ **teaspoon dried basil, crushed**
- 2 **cups seedless red grapes, whole and/or halved**
- 1 **tablespoon snipped fresh rosemary**
- 1 **tablespoon grated Romano cheese**

1 Let pizza dough stand at room temperature for 15 minutes. On a lightly floured surface, roll dough to 12x8-inch rectangle. If dough begins to pull back while rolling, let rest for 5 minutes. Transfer dough to lightly oiled baking sheet. Prick with fork. Cover; let rise in warm place for 30 minutes.

2 Preheat oven to 450°F. Brush dough with 1 tablespoon of the olive oil; sprinkle with salt and basil. Arrange grapes over dough; sprinkle with rosemary and cheese. Bake for 20 to 22 minutes or until puffed and lightly browned. Drizzle with remaining oil. Cut into strips with a pizza cutter or large knife.

Nutrition facts per serving: 111 cal., 4 g total fat (1 g sat. fat), 0 mg chol., 208 mg sodium, 17 g carb., 1 g dietary fiber, 2 g protein.

focaccia BREADSTICKS

Prep: 15 minutes
Bake: 12 minutes
Makes: 16 servings

¼ cup oil-packed sun-dried tomatoes

¼ cup grated Romano cheese

2 teaspoons water

⅛ teaspoon cracked black pepper

1 10-ounce package refrigerated pizza dough

1 Preheat oven to 350°F. Drain dried tomatoes, reserving oil; finely snip tomatoes. In a bowl, combine tomatoes, 2 teaspoons of the reserved oil, the cheese, water, and pepper.

2 Unroll the pizza dough. On a lightly floured surface, roll the dough into a 10x8-inch rectangle. Spread the tomato mixture crosswise over half of the dough. Fold plain half of dough over filling; press lightly to seal edges. Cut the folded dough crosswise into sixteen ½-inch strips. Twist each strip two or three times. Place 1 inch apart on a lightly greased baking sheet. Bake for 12 to 15 minutes or until golden brown. Cool on a wire rack.

Nutrition facts per serving: 84 cal., 2 g total fat (1 g sat. fat), 2 mg chol., 209 mg sodium, 14 g carb., 1 g dietary fiber, 3 g protein.

tomato-basil PANINI

Prep: 20 minutes
Cook: 2 minutes per batch
Makes: 4 servings

8 slices whole wheat bread;
four 6-inch whole wheat
hoagie rolls, split; or
2 whole wheat pita
bread rounds, halved
crosswise and split
horizontally

4 cups baby spinach leaves

1 medium tomato, cut in
8 slices

⅛ teaspoon salt

⅛ teaspoon ground black
pepper

¼ cup thinly sliced red
onion

2 tablespoons shredded
fresh basil

½ cup crumbled reduced-fat
feta cheese (2 ounces)

1 Lightly coat an unheated electric sandwich press, panini griddle, covered indoor grill, grill pan, or large nonstick skillet with nonstick cooking spray; set aside.

2 Place 4 of the bread slices, roll bottoms, or pita pieces on a work surface; divide half of the spinach leaves among these bread slices, roll bottoms, or pita pieces. Top spinach with tomato; sprinkle lightly with salt and pepper. Add red onion and basil. Top with feta and the remaining spinach. Top with the remaining bread slices, roll tops, or pita pieces. Press down firmly.

3 Preheat sandwich press, panini griddle, or covered indoor grill according to manufacturer's directions. (Or heat grill pan or skillet over medium heat.) Add sandwiches, in batches if necessary. If using sandwich press, panini griddle, or covered indoor grill, close lid and grill for 2 to 3 minutes or until bread is toasted. (If using grill pan or skillet, place a heavy skillet on top of sandwiches. Cook over medium heat for 1 to 2 minutes or until bottoms are toasted. Carefully remove top skillet, which may be hot. Turn sandwiches and top again with the skillet. Cook for 1 to 2 minutes more or until bread is toasted.)

Nutrition facts per serving: 174 cal., 5 g total fat (2 g sat. fat), 5 mg chol., 597 mg sodium, 27 g carb., 5 g dietary fiber, 10 g protein.

tarragon TUNA MELTS

Prep: 25 minutes
Cook: 6 minutes
Makes: 4 servings

⅓ **cup mayonnaise or salad dressing**

3 **tablespoons snipped fresh Italian parsley**

2 **tablespoons snipped fresh chives**

1 **to 2 tablespoons snipped fresh tarragon, or 2 teaspoons dried tarragon, crushed**

1 **teaspoon finely shredded lemon zest**

2 **teaspoons lemon juice**

1 **teaspoon Dijon-style mustard**

⅛ **teaspoon ground black pepper**

1 **12-ounce can solid white tuna (water pack), drained and flaked**

8 **½-inch-thick slices sourdough bread**

8 **to 12 thin tomato slices (optional)**

4 **ounces sharp white cheddar cheese, shredded (1 cup)**

2 **tablespoons butter, softened**

1 In a medium bowl, combine mayonnaise, parsley, chives, tarragon, lemon zest, lemon juice, mustard, and pepper; stir until well combined. Stir in tuna, breaking up any large pieces with a fork.

2 Place 4 bread slices on work surface; evenly divide tuna mixture among bread slices. Top each with tomato, if desired, and cheese. Spread one side of remaining bread slices with half the butter. Place bread slices, buttered side up, on top of cheese. Place sandwiches, buttered side down, on a large nonstick griddle over medium heat. Carefully butter top bread slices. Cook sandwiches for 6 to 8 minutes or until cheese is melted and bread is golden, carefully turning once halfway through cooking. (Or cook sandwiches, half at a time, in a large nonstick skillet.) Serve warm.

Nutrition facts per serving: 550 cal., 34 g total fat (12 g sat. fat), 95 mg chol., 988 mg sodium, 27 g carb., 2 g dietary fiber, 32 g protein.

portobello FOCACCIA SANDWICHES

Start to Finish: 25 minutes
Oven: Broil
Makes: 4 servings

1 **12-inch round garlic Italian flatbread (focaccia)**

4 **large fresh portobello mushroom caps, stems and gills removed**

2 **tablespoons olive oil**

2 **tablespoons balsamic vinegar**

¼ **cup purchased basil pesto**

2 **to 4 tablespoons mayonnaise**

⅛ **teaspoon ground black pepper**

1 **cup bottled roasted sweet red pepper strips, drained (optional)**

3 **ounces Fontina cheese, thinly sliced**

2 **cups arugula or spinach leaves**

1 Preheat broiler. Split focaccia in half horizontally. Place bread halves, cut sides up, on large baking sheet. Broil 4 to 5 inches from the heat for 3 to 4 minutes or until lightly toasted. Cool slightly.

2 Arrange mushroom caps on unheated rack of broiler pan. In a small bowl, whisk together oil and vinegar. Brush over both sides of mushroom caps. Broil for 8 to 10 minutes or until tender, turning once halfway through broiling time; cool slightly.

3 Meanwhile, spread cut side of the bottom bread half with pesto. Spread cut side of top bread half with mayonnaise. Sprinkle mayonnaise with black pepper.

4 Transfer mushrooms to cutting board. Cut each mushroom into quarters; arrange quarters on top of pesto. Top with roasted red pepper strips. Top with cheese. If desired return to broiler; broil for about 1 minute or until cheese melts. Add arugula and top bread half. Cut sandwich into quarters.

Nutrition facts per serving: 572 cal., 31 g total fat (10 g sat. fat), 31 mg chol., 308 mg sodium, 57 g carb., 6 g dietary fiber, 21 g protein.

stuffed FOCACCIA

Makes: 3 servings

½ **of a 9- to 10-inch garlic,
onion, or plain Italian
flatbread (focaccia),
split horizontally**

½ **of an 8-ounce container
mascarpone cheese**

1 **6-ounce jar marinated
artichoke hearts, drained
and chopped**

1 **tablespoon capers,
drained (optional)**

4 **ounces thinly sliced
Genoa salami**

1 **cup arugula leaves**

1 Spread cut sides of focaccia with mascarpone cheese. Sprinkle bottom half of focaccia with artichoke hearts and, if desired, capers; top with salami and arugula leaves. Add top of focaccia, cheese side down.

2 Cut sandwich into thirds. Serve immediately or chill for up to 4 hours before serving.

Nutrition facts per serving: 545 cal., 36 g total fat (16 g sat. fat), 83 mg chol., 970 mg sodium, 43 g carb., 3 g dietary fiber, 23 g protein.

italian PROSCIUTTO AND CHEESE SANDWICHES

Prep: 15 minutes
Bake: 15 minutes
Oven: 350°F
Makes: 4 servings

- 1 4.5- to 5-ounce round Brie cheese
- 1 1-pound loaf French bread
- 1½ cups coarsely chopped roma tomatoes
- 1 cup coarsely chopped prosciutto or cooked ham
- 2 tablespoons olive oil
- 1 teaspoon dried oregano, crushed
- 2 cloves garlic, minced
- ½ cup finely shredded Italian-blend cheese (2 ounces)
- 2 tablespoons balsamic vinegar

① Preheat oven to 350°F. If desired, use a vegetable peeler to remove edible rind from Brie. Cut Brie into cubes; set aside.

② Split French bread horizontally in half. Hollow out one of the bread halves, leaving a ½-inch shell. Place hollowed bread half, cut side up, on a baking sheet. (Save remaining bread for another use.)

③ In a medium bowl, toss together tomatoes, prosciutto, oil, oregano, garlic, and Brie; spoon into hollowed bread half. Sprinkle with shredded cheese. Bake for about 15 minutes or until heated through. Drizzle with vinegar. To serve, cut crosswise into 4 portions.

Nutrition facts per serving: 618 cal., 26 g total fat (10 g sat. fat), 66 mg chol., 1541 mg sodium, 66 g carb., 5 g dietary fiber, 28 g protein.

bacon AND EDAMAME WRAPS

This hearty wrap offers all the wonderful flavors of a BLT with extra protein from the soybeans and extra kick from the jalapeño chile pepper.

Start to Finish: 30 minutes
Makes: 4 servings

½ of a 10- to 12-ounce package fresh or thawed frozen sweet soybeans (edamame; about 1 cup)

1 medium fresh jalapeño chile pepper, seeded and chopped*

2 tablespoons snipped fresh cilantro

2 tablespoons lemon juice

2 tablespoons water

1 clove garlic, halved

4 slices soy bacon or turkey bacon

4 8-inch whole wheat flour tortillas or vegetable-flavored flour tortillas

2 cups torn mixed salad greens

2 medium tomatoes, seeded and chopped

1 If necessary, cook edamame according to package directions. Drain; rinse with cold water. Drain again. In a food processor, combine edamame, jalapeño, cilantro, lemon juice, the water, and garlic. Cover and process until smooth. Set aside.

2 Cook bacon according to package directions. Drain well on paper towels. Chop bacon.

3 To assemble, spread about ¼ cup of the edamame mixture on each tortilla. Top with salad greens, tomatoes, and bacon, placing these ingredients on edge of each tortilla. Roll up to enclose filling. Secure with a toothpick or wrap bottoms in plastic wrap or foil to hold together. Cut in half to serve.

Nutrition facts per serving: 222 cal., 7 g total fat (1 g sat. fat), 0 mg chol., 502 mg sodium, 24 g carb., 13 g dietary fiber, 16 g protein.

*Tip: Because chile peppers contain volatile oils that can burn your skin and eyes, avoid direct contact with them as much as possible. When working with chile peppers, wear plastic or rubber gloves. If your bare hands do touch the peppers, wash your hands and nails well with soap and warm water.

veggie-hummus WRAPS

The secret to vegetable wraps is to cut the vegetables thinly so they will roll up.

Start to Finish: 25 minutes
Makes: 6 servings

1   small cucumber

¾   cup hummus or flavored hummus

6   9- to 10-inch spinach-flavored flour tortillas or whole wheat flatbread

1   cup shredded romaine lettuce or spinach

1   medium tomato, thinly sliced

½   cup thinly sliced red onion

2   ounces goat cheese, crumbled

1 Trim the ends from the cucumber, then using a sharp vegetable peeler, shave the cucumber lengthwise into thin ribbons, discarding seeds; set aside. Spread hummus evenly over one side of each tortilla.

2 In a large bowl, toss together cucumber, lettuce, tomato, red onion, and goat cheese. Divide vegetable mixture among tortillas. Starting at the bottom of the wrap, roll into a tight spiral. Slice in half on the diagonal; serve.

Nutrition facts per serving: 306 cal., 10 g total fat (3 g sat. fat), 7 mg chol., 500 mg sodium, 43 g carb., 5 g dietary fiber, 10 g protein.

roasted PEPPER AND GOAT CHEESE SANDWICHES

To save time, ingredients can be prepped a day ahead and then assembled the day of serving.

Prep: 1 hour
Marinate: 4 hours
Assemble: 10 minutes
Oven: 500°F
Makes: 4 to 6 servings

- 4 large red or yellow sweet peppers
- 2 tablespoons extra-virgin olive oil
- 1 tablespoon balsamic vinegar
- 2 cloves garlic, minced
- 2 teaspoons kosher salt
- 1 teaspoon ground black pepper
- 2 tablespoons drained jarred capers
- 1 1-pound loaf ciabatta, halved horizontally
- 1 11-ounce log soft garlic-and-herb or plain goat cheese, at room temperature
- 8 to 10 large fresh basil leaves
- 3 thin slices red onion

1 Preheat oven to 500°F. On a baking sheet, arrange sweet peppers in a single layer and roast, turning twice, until skins are completely wrinkled and charred, 30 to 40 minutes. Remove from oven and immediately cover baking sheet tightly with foil. Let stand until peppers are cool enough to handle, about 30 minutes.

2 Meanwhile, in a small bowl whisk together oil, vinegar, garlic, salt, and black pepper until well combined.

3 Remove and discard stems from peppers and quarter each. Remove and discard peels and seeds; transfer to a bowl along with any juices. Pour oil-and-vinegar mixture over peppers; stir in capers. Cover with plastic wrap and marinate in the refrigerator at least 4 hours or overnight.

4 To assemble sandwiches, spread cut side of bottom half of ciabatta with goat cheese. Add a layer of peppers, then a layer of basil leaves. Separate onion slices into rings and spread out over basil; season with salt and pepper. Cover with top half of ciabatta and cut into individual servings.

Nutrition facts per serving (based on 5 servings): 510 cal., 22 g total fat (10.5 g sat. fat), 29 mg chol., 1639 mg sodium, 55 g carb., 5 g dietary fiber, 21 g protein.

spinach-berry SALAD

⅓ cup bottled reduced-calorie raspberry vinaigrette

1 teaspoon finely shredded orange zest

1 tablespoon orange juice

8 cups packaged baby spinach or torn mixed salad greens

3 cups sliced fresh strawberries and/or whole blueberries

¼ cup coarsely chopped pecans, toasted

1 For dressing, in a small bowl stir together vinaigrette, orange zest, and orange juice.

2 Divide spinach and berries among salad plates. Drizzle with dressing and sprinkle with pecans.

Nutrition facts per serving: 72 cal., 4 g total fat (0 g sat. fat), 0 mg chol., 34 mg sodium, 10 g carb., 2 g dietary fiber, 2 g protein.

chopped SALAD

Start to Finish: 30 minutes
Makes: 8 servings

6   ounces romaine and/or
    iceberg lettuce

2   ounces arugula or spinach

12 ounces tomatoes

1   large yellow or red sweet
    pepper

1   medium red onion

4   ounces ricotta salata or
    feta cheese, cut into
    ¾-inch cubes

1   15-ounce can garbanzo
    beans (chickpeas), rinsed
    and drained

4   ounces salami, cut into
    ¾-inch cubes (optional)

½   cup pitted kalamata
    olives, halved

½   cup olive oil

3   tablespoons white wine
    vinegar

1   tablespoon Dijon-style
    mustard

½   teaspoon salt

¼   teaspoon ground black
    pepper

1 Chop romaine, arugula, tomatoes, sweet pepper, and onion into ¾-inch dice. Combine in a very large bowl with cheese, beans, salami (if desired), and olives.

2 In a small bowl, whisk together oil, vinegar, mustard, salt, and black pepper. Add to greens mixture; toss to coat.

Nutrition facts per serving: 264 cal., 19 g total fat (4 g sat. fat), 13 mg chol., 609 mg sodium, 19 g carb., 4 g dietary fiber, 6 g protein.

honey-mustard FRUIT SLAW

Traditional coleslaw gets a makeover with an added twist of apple or pear and homemade honey-mustard dressing.

Prep: 20 minutes
Chill: 2 hours
Makes: 2 servings

¾ **cup shredded green cabbage**

½ **cup shredded carrot**

⅓ **cup coarsely chopped apple or pear**

2 **teaspoons salad oil**

2 **teaspoons Dijon-style mustard or coarse-grain brown mustard**

1½ **teaspoons lemon juice**

1½ **teaspoons honey**

1 **small clove garlic, minced**

1 **tablespoon chopped peanuts or cashews**

1 In a medium bowl, toss together cabbage, carrot, and apple.

2 For dressing, in a small screw-top jar combine salad oil, mustard, lemon juice, honey, and garlic. Cover and shake well. Pour dressing over cabbage mixture; toss gently to coat. Cover and refrigerate for 2 to 24 hours.

3 Before serving, sprinkle the cabbage mixture with peanuts.

Nutrition facts per serving: 118 cal., 7 g total fat (1 g sat. fat), 0 mg chol., 181 mg sodium, 13 g carb., 2 g dietary fiber, 2 g protein.

tomato BREAD SALAD

Prep: 35 minutes
Bake: 10 minutes
Stand: 1 hour
Oven: 400°F
Makes: 6 to 8 servings

4 medium roma tomatoes, cut into 1-inch chunks

½ of a medium red onion, cut into thin wedges (½ cup)

1 medium yellow sweet pepper, cut into 1-inch pieces

¼ cup olive oil

¼ cup red wine vinegar

1 tablespoon Dijon-style mustard

½ teaspoon Italian seasoning, crushed

½ teaspoon salt

¼ teaspoon ground black pepper

8 ounces ciabatta or focaccia bread, cut into 1-inch pieces

1 tablespoon olive oil

1 cup small fresh basil leaves

White cheddar cheese shavings (optional)

1 In a large bowl, combine tomatoes, red onion, and sweet pepper. In a screw-top jar, combine ¼ cup olive oil, the red wine vinegar, mustard, Italian seasoning, salt, and black pepper. Cover; shake well to combine. Add to tomato mixture and stir to coat. Cover and refrigerate overnight (up to 24 hours).

2 Preheat oven to 400°F. In a shallow baking pan, toss bread cubes with 1 tablespoon olive oil to coat. Bake for about 10 minutes or until toasted, stirring once. Remove and cool on pan. Add bread cubes and basil to tomato mixture; toss to coat. Top with shaved cheese.

Nutrition facts per serving: 225 cal., 13 g total fat (3 g sat. fat), 0 mg chol., 453 mg sodium, 23 g carb., 3 g dietary fiber, 5 g protein.

Make-Ahead Directions: Cube the bread and place in an airtight container. Cover and store at room temperature for up to 24 hours. Toss with oil and toast as directed.

corn BREAD SALAD

Prep: 20 minutes
Bake: 20 minutes
Chill: 2 to 24 hours
Oven: 400°F
Makes: 10 to 12 servings

1 **8.5-ounce package corn muffin mix**

1 **cup mayonnaise or salad dressing**

1 **8-ounce carton sour cream**

1 **0.4-ounce envelope dry ranch salad dressing mix**

2 **15-ounce cans pinto beans, rinsed and drained**

1 **15.25-ounce can whole kernel corn, drained**

1 **cup chopped tomatoes (2 medium)**

¾ **cup chopped green sweet pepper (1 medium)**

½ **cup sliced scallions**

8 **slices bacon, crisp-cooked, drained, and crumbled**

2 **cups shredded cheddar cheese (8 ounces)**

1 Preheat oven to 400°F. Grease an 8-inch ovenproof cast-iron skillet. Prepare muffin mix according to package directions. Spread batter in the prepared skillet. Bake, uncovered, for 20 to 25 minutes or until a toothpick inserted near the center comes out clean. Cool on a wire rack. Coarsely crumble corn bread; set aside.

2 For dressing, in a medium bowl combine mayonnaise, sour cream, and salad dressing mix. In a large bowl, combine beans, corn, tomatoes, sweet pepper, scallions, and bacon.

3 In a 3-quart glass bowl, layer half of the corn bread, half of the bean mixture, and half of the cheese. Spread half of the dressing over layers in bowl. Repeat layers. Cover and chill for 2 to 24 hours.

4 To serve, toss gently to coat corn bread and vegetables with dressing.

Nutrition facts per serving: 564 cal., 37 g total fat (13 g sat. fat), 68 mg chol., 1126 mg sodium, 38 g carb., 6 g dietary fiber, 16 g protein.

caesar SALAD

Prep: 30 minutes
Bake: 20 minutes
Oven: 300°F
Makes: 6 servings

3 cloves garlic

3 anchovy fillets

2 tablespoons lemon juice

¼ cup olive oil

1 teaspoon Dijon-style mustard

½ teaspoon sugar

1 hard-cooked egg yolk

1 clove garlic, halved

10 cups torn romaine

Parmesan Croutons* or 2 cups purchased garlic-Parmesan croutons

¼ cup grated Parmesan cheese, or ½ cup Parmesan shavings

Anchovy fillets, halved lengthwise (optional)

Ground black pepper

1 For dressing, in a blender combine the 3 garlic cloves, the 3 anchovy fillets, and lemon juice. Cover and blend until mixture is nearly smooth, stopping to scrape down sides as needed. Add oil, mustard, sugar, and cooked egg yolk. Cover and blend or process until smooth. Use immediately or cover and chill for up to 24 hours.

2 To serve, rub inside of a wooden salad bowl with cut edges of halved garlic clove; discard garlic clove. Add romaine and croutons to bowl. Pour dressing over salad; toss lightly to coat. Sprinkle Parmesan cheese over top; toss gently. Add anchovy fillets, if desired. To serve, divide salad among salad plates; sprinkle pepper over each salad.

*Parmesan Croutons: Preheat oven to 300°F. Cut four ¾-inch-thick slices Italian or French bread into 1-inch cubes (you should have about 3½ cups). In a small saucepan, melt ¼ cup butter. Remove from heat. Transfer to a large bowl. Stir in 3 tablespoons grated Parmesan cheese and 2 finely minced garlic cloves. Add bread cubes, stirring until cubes are coated with butter mixture. Spread bread cubes in a single layer in a shallow baking pan or on a baking sheet. Bake for 10 minutes; stir. Bake for about 10 minutes more or until bread cubes are crisp and golden. Cool completely; store in an airtight container for up to 24 hours.

Nutrition facts per serving: 261 cal., 20 g total fat (8 g sat. fat), 62 mg chol., 362 mg sodium, 15 g carb., 2 g dietary fiber, 6 g protein.

metric information

The charts on this page provide a guide for converting measurements from the U.S. customary system, which is used throughout this book, to the metric system.

PRODUCT DIFFERENCES

Most of the ingredients called for in the recipes in this book are available in most countries. However, some are known by different names. Here are some common American ingredients and their possible counterparts:

- Sugar (white) is granulated, fine granulated, or castor sugar.
- Powdered sugar is icing sugar.
- All-purpose flour is enriched, bleached, or unbleached white household flour. When self-rising flour is used in place of all-purpose flour in a recipe that calls for leavening, omit the leavening agent (baking soda or baking powder) and salt.
- Light-colored corn syrup is golden syrup.
- Cornstarch is cornflour.
- Baking soda is bicarbonate of soda.
- Vanilla or vanilla extract is vanilla essence.
- Green, red, or yellow sweet peppers are capsicums or bell peppers.
- Golden raisins are sultanas.

VOLUME AND WEIGHT

The United States traditionally uses cup measures for liquid and solid ingredients. The chart, top right, shows the approximate imperial and metric equivalents. If you are accustomed to weighing solid ingredients, the following approximate equivalents will be helpful.

- 1 cup butter, castor sugar, or rice = 8 ounces = $\frac{1}{2}$ pound = 250 grams
- 1 cup flour = 4 ounces = $\frac{1}{4}$ pound = 125 grams
- 1 cup icing sugar = 5 ounces = 150 grams

Canadian and U.S. volume for a cup measure is 8 fluid ounces (237 ml), but the standard metric equivalent is 250 ml.

1 British imperial cup is 10 fluid ounces.

In Australia, 1 tablespoon equals 20 ml, and there are 4 teaspoons in the Australian tablespoon.

Spoon measures are used for smaller amounts of ingredients. Although the size of the tablespoon varies slightly in different countries, for practical purposes and for recipes in this book, a straight substitution is all that's necessary. Measurements made using cups or spoons always should be level unless stated otherwise.

COMMON WEIGHT RANGE REPLACEMENTS

Imperial / U.S.	Metric
$\frac{1}{2}$ ounce	15 g
1 ounce	25 g or 30 g
4 ounces ($\frac{1}{4}$ pound)	115 g or 125 g
8 ounces ($\frac{1}{2}$ pound)	225 g or 250 g
16 ounces (1 pound)	450 g or 500 g
$1\frac{1}{4}$ pounds	625 g
$1\frac{1}{2}$ pounds	750 g
2 pounds or $2\frac{1}{4}$ pounds	1,000 g or 1 Kg

OVEN TEMPERATURE EQUIVALENTS

Fahrenheit Setting	Celsius Setting*	Gas Setting
300°F	150°C	Gas Mark 2 (very low)
325°F	160°C	Gas Mark 3 (low)
350°F	180°C	Gas Mark 4 (moderate)
375°F	190°C	Gas Mark 5 (moderate)
400°F	200°C	Gas Mark 6 (hot)
425°F	220°C	Gas Mark 7 (hot)
450°F	230°C	Gas Mark 8 (very hot)
475°F	240°C	Gas Mark 9 (very hot)
500°F	260°C	Gas Mark 10 (extremely hot)
Broil	Broil	Grill

*Electric and gas ovens may be calibrated using Celsius. However, for an electric oven, increase Celsius setting 10 to 20 degrees when cooking above 160°C. For convection or forced air ovens (gas or electric), lower the temperature setting 25°F/10°C when cooking at all heat levels.

BAKING PAN SIZES

Imperial / U.S.	Metric
9×1$\frac{1}{2}$-inch round cake pan	22- or 23×4-cm (1.5 L)
9×1$\frac{1}{2}$-inch pie plate	22- or 23×4-cm (1 L)
8×8×2-inch square cake pan	20×5-cm (2 L)
9×9×2-inch square cake pan	22- or 23×4.5-cm (2.5 L)
11×7×1$\frac{1}{2}$-inch baking pan	28×17×4-cm (2 L)
2-quart rectangular baking pan	30×19×4.5-cm (3 L)
13×9×2-inch baking pan	34×22×4.5-cm (3.5 L)
15×10×1-inch jelly roll pan	40×25×2-cm
9×5×3-inch loaf pan	23×13×8-cm (2 L)
2-quart casserole	2 L

U.S. / STANDARD METRIC EQUIVALENTS

$\frac{1}{8}$ teaspoon = 0.5 ml	$\frac{1}{3}$ cup = 3 fluid ounces = 75 ml
$\frac{1}{4}$ teaspoon = 1 ml	$\frac{1}{2}$ cup = 4 fluid ounces = 125 ml
$\frac{1}{2}$ teaspoon = 2 ml	$\frac{1}{3}$ cup = 5 fluid ounces = 150 ml
1 teaspoon = 5 ml	$\frac{3}{4}$ cup = 6 fluid ounces = 175 ml
1 tablespoon = 15 ml	1 cup = 8 fluid ounces = 250 ml
2 tablespoons = 25 ml	2 cups = 1 pint = 500 ml
$\frac{1}{4}$ cup = 2 fluid ounces = 50 ml	1 quart = 1 liter

index

Note: Page numbers in *italics* refer to photographs.

Z